LAFCADIO HEARN'S strange and colorful life led him finally to Japan, where he married a Japanese woman and became, as nearly as it was possible, himself a Japanese. Kazuo Koizumi is the son of the marriage. In this quaint and charming narrative, he pictures Hearn in an entirely new aspect — that of a father and family man. As the boy was only ten years old when Hearn died, the book deals entirely with his childhood memories of his father, of his own boyhood, and of the Hearn family life in various Japanese cities.

In addition to the invaluable light it throws on a side of Hearn that has never yet been revealed, 'Father and I' is an absorbing account of a typical Japanese childhood a quarter of a century ago during the transitional stage in Japan's evolution, written with an Oriental flavor all its own, a turn of phrase that is somewhat foreign to English and yet is infused with poetry and with humor. The book is illustrated with pen-sketches by Hearn and with a hitherto unpublished photograph of the Hearn family.

FATHER AND I

Memories of Lafcadio Hearn

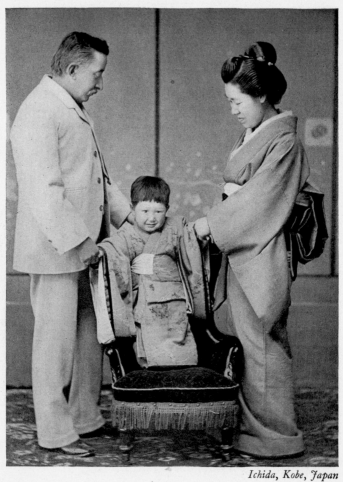

Ichida, Kobe, Japan

LAFCADIO HEARN WITH HIS WIFE AND SON KAZUO AT
KUMAMOTO, 1895

FATHER AND I

Memories of Lafcadio Hearn

by Kazuo
Koizumi

Boston and New York
HOUGHTON MIFFLIN COMPANY
The Riverside Press Cambridge
1935

The Riverside Press
CAMBRIDGE · MASSACHUSETTS
PRINTED IN THE U.S.A.

TO

DR. YONEKO YANAGISAWA

Publishers' Note

KAZUO KOIZUMI, the eldest son of Lafcadio Hearn, was not quite eleven years old when his father died. His most vivid memories are of the last period of Hearn's career, when he held the position of Professor of English at the Imperial University of Tōkyo. Possessing all the keenness, the unstudied charm, of childhood observations, they at once sharpen and complete our picture of America's supreme prose stylist and the greatest interpreter of Japan to the Western world.

Hearn came to Japan for the first time in the spring of 1890; he remained there for the rest of his life. In 1891, when he was teaching school in the town of Matsué, he married Setsuko Koizumi, a member of a distinguished Samurai family. To avoid the legal complications which his foreign citizenship might bring upon his family, he became a naturalized Japanese, adopting his wife's family name, Koizumi ('Little Spring').

The climate of Matsué proved too severe for Hearn's delicate health and he obtained a transfer to the Government College at Kumamoto, where Kazuo ('The first of the excellent, the best of the peerless') was born on November 17, 1893, the first of three sons and a daughter. Dissatisfied with teaching conditions at the Government College, Hearn returned the next year to his old calling of journalism, joining the staff of the Kobe *Chronicle*. The work affected his eyesight, however, and the income was scarcely sufficient for the support of his increasing household — he had, with his wife's relatives, thirteen people dependent on him. In 1896 he accepted the chair of English Literature at the Imperial University of Tōkyo, which he held until 1903. He died of a heart attack on September 26, 1904.

Contents

INTRODUCTION · 3

I.   BEFORE COMING TO TŌKYŌ   15

II. AT USHIGOMÉ   27

III. AT THE SEA   71

IV. MY LESSONS   127

V.   WALKS   167

VI. AT ŌKUBO   185

Illustrations

LAFCADIO HEARN WITH HIS WIFE AND SON KAZUO
AT KUMAMOTO, 1895   *Frontispiece*

PEN-SKETCHES BY LAFCADIO HEARN   32
   Hearn's Self-Portrait — Kazuo Swimming — A View of
   Yaidzu Bay

PEN-SKETCHES BY LAFCADIO HEARN   98
   A View of Yaidzu Bay — Yaidzu Fishermen — The
   Breakwater of Yaidzu

PEN-SKETCHES BY LAFCADIO HEARN   172
   The Weeping Jizō in Yaidzu — The Poor Mouse —
   Landing the Boat

FATHER AND I

Memories of Lafcadio Hearn

Introduction

A few years ago, on the occasion of the twenty-fifth anniversary of the death of my father, Lafcadio Hearn — or Yakumo Koizumi as he was called later in Japan — I was approached from many quarters to write something about him.

In Japan alone, many books have been published on his life, and his photograph, which he disliked to be looked upon, began to appear, not only in some of these publications, but even in advertisements of patent medicines. The saintly, seclusive father Yakumo has thus become very familiar to everyone. So to go over his life history is quite needless, nor have I the least desire to attempt anything of the sort.

I am sure there are many people who have been placed in the same difficult position as I, uncertain whether to speak or to keep silence. There is a saying, 'It is best not to disclose everything.' Then another, 'Eloquence is silver, silence is gold.' These are the expressions of troubled, undecided minds.

A certain Zen priest has said, 'To say it out deserves thirty thrashings, and not to say it out deserves thirty thrashings.' I seem to be in a position to receive the thrashings, whichever attitude I take.

There are some friends who urge me by saying: 'Many people make publicity of their parents, children, wives or husbands by advertising their titles, degrees, family history — as by a signboard — or think nothing of making known their private troubles to the world for the sake of their livelihood. There being such — you can do it too.' Misguided, ambitious people without any thought simply urge me, saying, 'Do it; do it without any hesitation.'

Of one thing I am certain, and that is, father loved me dearly and I loved him. So to those who ask me for reminiscences of my father, to them alone I should like to relate the story in my humble little room. But I am no hand at story-telling; I get nervous and stammer and am not capable of telling a story smoothly. So that is out of the question.

At any rate, I have decided to write something on my remembrance of my father. 'Like father, like son' — I am backward about speaking or writing; not only unaccustomed to it, but am an infant at it, and when this infant attempts anything, he is only moved by his feelings and goes out of his depth. Such a poor writer has been asked to write, so it will be no wonder if he makes a mess of it and spatters ink on the faces of some people.

Over sea and land, father Hearn has been written about. Some wrote with good intentions and some with bad; some worshipped him and some hated him; some wrote with jealousy, and some to make a name for themselves through this means. Whatever was said of him, it does not matter. One thing is certain, he loved Japan and was a friend of the Japanese.

I don't intend to defend my father nor do I care to abuse him. He had some traits which I admired and others that I disliked. My only desire is to write at random my impressions of him.

My father died when I was but ten years and ten months old, so my remembrance of him is but that of a child. I knew him only as a father at home, not as a serious lecturer or writer of essays. Moreover, my impressions of him are those of a very nervous child. I have tried to put by my later ideas of him and to give here my true childhood memories.

After father's death our family life became greatly changed, though outwardly all seemed well. The days that father was with us became dearer to us than ever, and I soon got into the habit of reflecting more and more on the past. After his death I discovered from his book, 'Out

of the East,' what father says about the Japanese
students: 'All this capacity of young men to turn
back with perfect naturalness of feeling to scenes
of their childhood appears to me essentially
Oriental. In the Occident men seldom begin to
recall their childhood vividly before the approach
of the autumn season of life. But childhood in
Japan is certainly happier than in other lands,
and therefore perhaps is regretted earlier in adult
life.' Whether it was because he had reached the
autumn of life or because he considered himself
one of the East, he very frequently took pleasure
in recollecting the past. He would often relate to
me with much pleasure incidents of his boyhood
days, recalling his struggles and hardships like
an interesting dream story. But he always avoided
recalling the worst ones. When mother would
tell of the struggles that she experienced as a girl,
the abolition of the clan system which brought
such suffering to the Samurai class, father would
always check her with 'Don't say any more!'

As I grew older, father tried to keep me by him
more and more. He was my instructor in reading,
composition, writing; in swimming and gymnastics. His near-sightedness prevented him from
taking part in any vigorous sports, but he did not
dislike them. He took considerable interest in
exercise, and used to swing twenty-pound dumb-
bells himself. A walk of two or three *ri* (five or
six miles) in the country was nothing to him.

In summer vacations we used to go bathing in the sea at Yaidzu in Shizuoka Prefecture. On father's desk I often saw sketches of muscular arms; he seemed to admire a robust physique. He thought that every healthy person should take pleasure in some sort of sport, whether young or old. But to go into sports too deeply — to injure one's life — that he deplored.

Father used to say, 'No boy or girl should ever be left unguarded.' If he could have seen a 'modern' girl, he would have been shocked more than by the great earthquake. Even to parents and children, brothers and sisters, husbands and wives, teachers and pupils, he would say: Bad is bad, and should be punished. The guilty one should be made to repent or resort to forced suicide even if he be one's own child or kinsman. Father thus showed his admiration for the true ancestral blood of the Japanese.

Any misconduct or unkind act on the part of his children he would never tolerate or let pass with soft words. The misdoings of young girls or boys he might attribute to their youth; but when fathers and mothers deserted their own wives and husbands to live with others, his disgust for them was beyond expression. Today such people take delight in writing up their disgrace in the magazines and newspapers, as if they had done something great, under the title of 'My Past Life' or 'My True Confession,' and so forth. At the sight of stories like that, my father would surely have lost consciousness. He died at a good time.

Father used to admire the dwarf plants, but he pitied them. Potted plants, caged birds and insects, he would let free almost always in our garden. He loved to live near to nature. Whenever we were at the Yaidzu seashore, he would always go in bathing nude. He would eat fruit without paring the skin whenever it was possible. He never wore glasses nor used artificial teeth.

Father thought he liked freedom and nature. His freedom, however, was the freedom of moral etiquette — and not freedom as understood today. He disliked such characters as Tōjin Okichi or Madam Chrysanthemum. He would not praise the act of a woman who would rather die than have any illicit relation with a foreigner and die uttering words of patriotism. Women whom father liked were the heroine Kimiko in his 'Kokoro' or 'The Woman's Diary' in 'Kotto.' And he also sympathized with Hatakeyama Yūko.

Even nowadays we frequently hear Admiral Tōgō praised as the Nelson of the Orient. Father disliked such comparison. He died without hearing of the victory of the Japan Sea, but he had anticipated that such result would take place before very long and he used to kiss the picture of Admiral Tōgō and ask him to please win. When this same expression was applied to Rear-Admiral Uryu and Commander Hirose, he would say,

'Nelson did a great thing for Britain, but if he had been morally perfect, Englishmen would have shown more pride to the world. Hirose was prepared for death, so he would not marry. Nelson knew that he must die to accomplish his aim, so he indulged in immoral things. There is a great difference between these two characters. Hirose, Uryu, Tōgō — these were noble Bushi (or Samurai) of Japan. To compare them with Nelson would be lowering the characters of these fine Japanese and disgracing them.'

Just as in Europe or America, father had great sympathy for the widows. So soon after he came to Japan, there was a seducing widow who came to gain his sympathy. Father with his one eye was able to take her in, so he escaped from the web which she had spun for him.

Father always sympathized with lonely, sad women, but never in any intimate sense. If a woman had been unhappily mated to a reckless adopted son, or married to an immoral man and plagued by his family, or married happily but had lost her husband — if she were still young and pretty, he always advised her to remarry. But on the contrary, the widows who pretended to be mourning for their departed husbands and carried on flirtations and led a shameful life — these he hated as cowardly liars and used to say that they were doomed for the bottom of hell. Of such a nature was my father that he always praised the widows who wished to follow their husbands in death or the husbands who grieved for their dead wives. He had no sympathy whatever with those who committed double suicide with another man's wife, asking to be buried together in a lovers' mound.

Father used to express his desire to write on Japanese 'No' (a type of drama) and the theatre. At the time when Dr. Tsubouchi was praising 'Ten-no-Amishima' of Chikamatsu, father was asked about translating them, with the view to introducing them to foreign countries. But the plot of the story, where a man leaves his wife and child to elope with another woman, was against his belief, so he declined to undertake it. Too moralistic father! These people who go to bars, dance halls, etc., would think him a rustic.

Father was of sensitive nature, easily moved but very firm in other respects, unlike those who read Comrade Karl Marx and change their lives accordingly at once. He showed his warm, tender feelings, not only toward his own family, but toward the grass by the wayside and the insects. He hated those who plagued the weak, or led lives of hypocrites. Crookedness of any sort he would never overlook. Wickedness, cowardice — these he detested.

We children, whenever we did anything cowardly or did not indulge in good play, would be severely scolded. Fidelity was always his constant god, so no matter whether it was a man of strength or a scholar, if he should be a coward or a hypocrite, father would without hesitation decline to have anything to do with him. He was very strict in his manners, but he would never flatter those he disliked. When he got angry, he would turn pale and exclaim, 'I'll slap off your head!' or, 'I'll cut off your head!' It was his habit, at night, to place an old-fashioned big pistol under his pillow. In Tennessee, he saw a man dig out the eyeballs of an innocent little kitten and throw it away. When he saw this, his anger was beyond control, so he fired several shots after the fellow and regretted afterwards that the shots went wild.

This same spirit of hating to see innocent things tormented increased as he grew older. In appearance he was like the spring ocean — serene — but one could not have imagined that within that soul existed such a firm strong rock as no great wave or whirlpool could move. Money or rank could not buy his straight mind.

To me, my morning and evening lessons seemed earnest and severe. Father always said: 'It is only necessary for a man to give his sons education enough to start them out in life; after that, they should look after themselves. It is not necessary to leave them any fortune. But as for his wife and daughter, it is necessary to make provision for them.' If father had lived until I had become a man, I might have been able to look after my parents. In order to accomplish his aim, father had always said that it was not good to bring up children in Japan. But to send three sons abroad and to leave a property for his wife and daughter was a great problem to a man who had no other source of income than a teacher's salary, royalties from books, and payments for his writings. I have repeatedly heard father's cry, 'Money!' 'Money!' 'Money!' — which seemed pitiable. 'I don't want money for myself,' he would say. 'I only want it for my wife and children.' He always said these things in a touching voice. I can even recall that voice now; it has been stamped upon my ear. Whenever I used to hear father utter these words, in my childish heart I had a premonition that he had not long to live and it used to make me feel sad.

Sad to say, father turned grey young, before his ambitions were realized, and he looked much older than his age at the time of his death. He had houses and property in Okubo, but these things were all in mother's name. These were but the means to lighten the burden for me, the heir. It was the means to educate us boys and support his wife and daughter. For extravagance and for pleasure — no.

Father having died so early, I could not go abroad. Until I was twenty-five I was a student, helping Mr. McDonald or Mrs. Wetmore in order to get my education.

Father, one day, remarked to mother about the bad results from marriage of close relatives. But inter-racial marriage produced bad results too, he thought. He was thinking of writing on the subject to a foreign paper. When he consulted his wife, she replied, 'You are a product of inter-racial marriage — but are you a poor product?' He replied, 'At times I think I am a very poor result, almost a waste. This is a result of very distant inter-racial marriage, I think. So, I just thought that I would write about it.' 'But,' mother said, 'you write about such a thing, but you and I are two different races and what about our children? Is it right to acclaim to the world the poor product of such a marriage?' He said to her, 'Do you think so?' and he tore up his manuscript. I think of that manuscript now and imagine all sorts of things.

Father could not be a Japanese in feature — his large nose, face, skin — nor in language, but he was more than a real Japanese in the way he loved Japan. He knew Japanese mythology, legends, stories, poetry, songs, and folklore, and in these he was good. But on the other hand about Japanese politics, economic study, he did not know much. When such topics would come up, he always tried to avoid them by saying that he was an infant. He was blind to the common (debased) side of affairs. But about the future of Japan and its administrative policy, he was very much concerned — more so than people thought.

Two or three years before he passed away, father tried to keep me constantly near him, watching me closely in everything that I did, no matter how simple or trivial. If he thought that by explaining, I could be made to understand or to take interest in a thing — a larva on a branch of a tree, a drop of dew on a blade of grass, a grain of sand, or an ant carrying things, he would try to tell me all he knew about it. He never felt it troublesome. Perhaps that explains why, though I lost father early, I can recall very vividly his character, speech, and manners.

I

BEFORE COMING TO TŌKYO

I

BEFORE COMING TO TŌKYO

My FATHER was very loving but very severe; his severity made him the more endearing. In my relations with him I was like the people who live at the foot of a volcano, such as Mount Asama. Each morning and evening is displayed a new and charming aspect of the mountain, but all at once it will send up huge columns of fire and emit voluminous heavy stones from its quiet cone, the sight of which can never be erased from one's memory.

In my early days I was taken about on trains and boats, of which I was very fond, to Kumamoto, Kōbe, Kyōtō, Ōsaka, Idzumo, Isé, Tōkyo. One night at Kōbe, father and mother took me in a rickshaw to see the return of our triumphant troops from the Sino-Japanese War. The shouting of glad 'Banzais' reverberated in the air. At a distance, one could see only the boys' besmeared

faces and hands and they seemed simply dirty
soldiers, but a closer look revealed, under their
neglected, unshaven faces, brave spirits, respond-
ing to our 'Banzais' plodding along leading their
poor lean horses — marching, marching, one after
another. Such a procession of them! It was
hard to tell where they came from or where they
were going, and there seemed to be no end to the
column. The impression made on me at this time
is still very vivid, but some ten years later, when
I witnessed another triumphal return of our troops
after the Russo-Japanese War, the appearance of
the soldiers and the surrounding atmosphere did
not seem quite the same, that was certain. On
this occasion, among the crowd was an old woman, weeping and wandering about, scanning the
faces of the boys. Mother stopped and gave her
some money and tried to cheer her. That old
woman, I afterward learned, after looking eagerly
among the returned boys, was unable to find the
face of her son whom she thought ought to be
among them. That was why she was weeping.

On our way home father bought me a toy gun.
As we passed through the gaily lighted streets
hung with many round bright lanterns under the
eaves, I was soon fast asleep in the rickshaw,
sitting on mother's lap. I can never forget the
picture father made that night as he stood on the
floor of his rickshaw, eagerly scanning the scene,
holding the glass over his good eye and studying

the faces of the lively soldiers as they passed by him one by one. It is all so vivid!

While father was engaged as a teacher in the Matsué Middle and Normal Schools, among the teachers was one who had acted as go-between for father and mother, Mr. Sentaro Nishida, considered the Saint of Matsué. No one ever uttered a bad word against him. Besides Mr. Nishida, there were other teachers — more than half — whose characters father admired. Among them, however, were some with no reserve. Before father was married to mother, while he was living in a hotel, one of these frank teachers used to call on him. 'Today, I'm going to make Fellon [Matsué way of pronouncing Hearn] treat.' So saying, he would come abruptly into father's presence, shouting as he entered, 'Fellon, are you in?' He would bring up about twenty eggs and five bottles of *saké*, drink and eat them all alone at father's expense, at the same time whacking away on the edge of father's precious Chinese brazier and making dents on it with his hard metal-bowled tobacco pipe. When leaving, he would say, 'Many *sank* you I will come *tsu-morrow* again, *God-by*.' Using such Matsué English, he would depart pigeon-toed. This was of frequent occurrence at that time, so father's salary of one hundred yen did not go very far.

Mr. Yaichi Nakayama, formerly an English

teacher and a dormitory inspector at Matsué
Normal School, was another frequent visitor. He
both engaged in foreign trade and kept a curio
store under the name of Gyokusuido, dealing in
native agates, crystals, and other art objects.
Nakayama and his wife were a jolly good couple
and used to pet me a great deal. I saw them every
day while we lived in Kōbe. Auntie Nakayama
would make me some Japanese *gomokusushi* (rice
mixed with several kinds of vegetables). Nakayama's experience as a dormitory inspector was
not made up of a bed-of-roses, it seems, for he
used to remark frequently that he would never
consent to his sons or grandsons ever becoming
dormitory inspectors.

At Mihonoseki, in the hotel where we stopped
were two children older than I. They were
interested and respected me and wanted to please
me very much. After seeing father kiss me a number of times, they would try to practise the art on
me with their dirty nose-besmeared faces, which
affection I could not embrace. Every morning as
the mist or cloud rose from the mountains, they
would point to the famous 'Five Pines' [1] as they
came into view in the distance and exclaim, 'Botchan, come quick! You can see the Five Pines.'
And I would contradict them, saying, 'You're
wrong, it's only "four pines." At which remark

[1] See 'At Mionoseki' of Lafcadio Hearn's *Glimpses of Unfamiliar
Japan*, vol. I.

they would give in and say, 'Then it's "four pines."' I would continue to tantalize them, saying, 'No, it's *meotomatsu* (husbands' and wives' pines),' for I enjoyed the fun of teasing them. Physically, they were my superiors, but they could not get the better of me in arguments, but would take them in a good spirit, and it made me feel good.

Here we were with Mr. Tamura, who was with us later at Yaizu and Kugenuma. He would carry me on his shoulder and walk through the streets of the port. One day, while I was being carried in this usual manner, we passed a house where there were many women lying about on the floor. They beckoned for us to come, so coming up to a window with *sudare* (bamboo blinds), Tamura thrust me in through the window. I was surrounded by thickly powdered women and given wafers in the shape of wild geese, rice gruel containing salted sesame, etc. After thrusting me through the window, Tamura returned alone to the hotel. When asked, 'Where is Kazuo?' by father, he replied, 'He is now surrounded by the beauty group and very happy'; so saying he broke out in a loud 'Ha! Ha! Ha!' Hearing this, father exclaimed excitedly, 'I don't want my darling boy handled by those unclean women, most of whom must have dangerous diseases — more dreadful than the dirty noses of the boys of this hotel. Hurry quickly, someone, and get him!' I have never had but that one experience, before or since then, of being handled by such women.

If father was the chief actor, there were many sub-actors in our family. My great-grandfather by adoption was more than eighty years old and very active. In the summer when I was four, my parents took me to Matsué, and he was delighted to play with me. In the heat of midday, he would wander out with his high wooden clogs to buy something to please me. When young, he had been a caretaker of a young lord, so though he liked children very much, he was in some respects quite severe. During the Civil War he experienced many hardships (owing to the sudden changes in classes), went into business a number of times, and failed. He was eccentric in some respects. Even though he had no means to buy rice, no matter whether it was spring, summer, autumn, or winter (rain or shine), he always wore his white *tabi* (socks) except when asleep. If someone called at the door, he would shout out in a gruff voice, 'Who are you!' At Kumamoto I was told he lived with us about a year. When father rented a house at Tetorimachi, great-grandfather looked around and selected the best room and announced, in a very serious voice, 'This is my room!' At Kumamoto, ice-sellers used to come in summer crying out, 'Ice! Ice!' He would stop and ask them in a serious manner, 'Did it come from Mount Hōkinodaisen?' which was many hundred miles away. When he missed a train once, he asked them to stop the train, as his grand-daughter and her husband were on that train, making such funny remarks at the station. Again at Mihonoseki, when he thought he had forgotten his tobacco pouch, he made the steamship go back after it, but in fact the pouch was on his person, having got around from his front to the back.

The morning I was born, he rushed to my father's study shouting, 'Hellum, great treasure child is born!' and waving his fist, with sleeves rolled up, he went around shouting, with tears of joy in his eyes. Such was our eccentric comical great-grandfather. He delighted to carry me about when an infant, singing loudly:

> Urashima Taro lived one hundred and six years
> Takeuchi Sukuné lived three hundred years,
> Tōbōsaku lived nine thousand years,
> Koizumi Kazuo — Ban-bansai!
>   (million and more million years)

This was something of his own composition and chantingly sung, like a priest, in a loud voice. His yawn was very peculiar, languid and long drawn out (and catching), somewhat sad-sounding, but could be heard in every room of the house. Every time father heard this yawn, he remarked smilingly, 'There's great-grandfather. Ah, that tired-of-the-world yawn of his again.'

Meiji 29 (1896) father severed his connection with the Kōbe *Chronicle* and came up to Tōkyo

to become a professor at the Imperial University.
We went to Isé in February, I am told. At this
time I did not seem to be in good spirits, and for
some reason or other would not leave my mother's
dark-cloaked back. Still, I have dim remembrance
of the grey-coloured waves through the misty
veil at Futamigaura. In Isé I was bought various
kinds of toys. On such occasions father and mother
held long consultations as to whether or not the
toy I desired was a proper selection. They would
try to find out why I wanted it, whether it was
too elegant or poorly made and unsafe; and the
discussion frequently resulted in my having to
give it up. If there was no danger and the toy
was very artistically made and I liked it, then,
even though it was expensive, my father never
hesitated to buy it for me. At such times mother
would remonstrate about such extravagance, but
her objections would be disregarded.

Such was the case with a black wooden horse at
Isé. 'Is the horse good for Kazuo's plaything?
What do you think of it?' father asked mother,
and mother said, 'We have bought so many
different kinds of toys ——' 'No, no! I am not
asking you about the other toys. Is that horse
good for him?' father repeated, and mother said,
'It is too good.' That was enough. There were
only about fifteen or sixteen minutes before the
train was to start, but father rushed off in a rickshaw from the station and went through the town

to the store and bought the big grand black horse and came back holding it up high on his knees just as the train was ready to pull out. That wooden horse could not have been found in any other store in Isé. The store that sold it, the rickshaw-man who pulled father, the people standing at the station gate and on the platform, all exclaimed, 'The finest in Isé! The finest in Isé!' This big strong black horse was taken to Kōbe and then to Tōkyo, and almost every day I rode on its back.

When in Kumamoto, father would buy from Kōbe or Yokohama a toy sheep that would move its head and bleat, a cow that would moo — such rare toys and baby carriages he would send for! All of these, with the exception of the cow, I kept until I was about fifteen or sixteen years. People seeing me being pushed in a baby carriage with a long string of sheep, cows, and other toys, a boat with a roof gaily decorated with red ball-like lanterns, would rush out. Little children of the neighbourhood and mothers followed in the procession, making quite a strange sight. This I faintly recollect as in a dream.

Looking over a collection of father's old letters, Kazuo (my name) was mentioned more than that of my mother, brothers, sister, or any other member of the family — much to my chagrin. Father always gave his special attention to me and I was never out of his thought.

II

AT USHIGOMÉ

II

AT USHIGOMÉ

In the autumn of 1896 we moved from Kōbe
to Tōkyo, where father was to teach English at
the Imperial University. While looking for a
house in the neighbourhood, father put up at
Hotel Tatsuoka. At last we settled on a house
at Tomihisacho, Ushigomé District, about three
miles from the University. We lived here till the
spring of 1902.

Back of the house which father rented was a
field of many acres. Beyond this field was an
old temple, which was known by its common
name of 'Kobudera' (meaning knotty temple),
and located on a hill. It may be strange to call it
a hill, or *yama*, but it was on an elevation behind
the field, thickly covered and dark with old trees,
even in the daytime, so the priests and other people
gave it the name 'Kobudera-no-Yama,' or the
hill of knotty temple. Pines, Japanese cedars,

pasania, oaks, zelkova trees, cypress, etc., of
unknown age, grew there, whose branches inter-
laced and cut off the sunshine. At the foot of
these trees were undergrowth of low stripped
bamboos, thorny hedges, sorrel vines, spear flower,
great plantain *mizuhikiso*, and other nameless
grasses (sometimes it seemed more appropriate to
call it a forest or a jungle), and this density continued until it came near to the Ichigaya Prison.
On spring mornings we could hear the joyous call
of the pheasants; in summer evenings, the lonely
hootings of owls. Crows made their nests among
the old stumps of the cedars, and snakes made
their homes in the old pines. On snowy days,
we could see rabbits happily hopping around the
ground, or on stormy nights hear the cries of foxes.

With this hill at our back, I played in the grass-
covered field with the children of the neighbourhood every day. Father used to take me frequently
to Kobudera, and very often the good old priest
patted me on the head. This temple was erected
in the year 1643 (Kanei 17) by the Daimyo of
Owari, in memory of his wife Jishō-in. The
materials for building this temple were all timbers
from knotty wood, purposely selected, whence it
derived its name of Kobudera. The temple
property was extensive, consisting of the hill
covered by old trees, a graveyard covered by old
tombs, and many acres of open space. Our rickshaw-man Nakamura rented a small portion of it

and raised for his family eggplants, cucumbers, pumpkins, corn, potatoes, radishes, carrots, and *gobo* (a kind of oyster plant). The products from this patch were quite sufficient to supply the wants of the family of five. 'Yes, come whenever you like,' was the cordial welcome from the priest, so father took the liberty of strolling around the hill, cemetery, temple garden, and compound whenever he found the gate open, and was free to come and go at will.

This priest, later transferred to Asakusa, was known as Archbishop Tatara. When he saw modern priests putting their robes and sutras in small modern suitcases, the Archbishop would ask in his ironical, joking manner, 'What have you in that Christian lunch box?' He was a true Tōkyoite, this priest. He was not able to speak freely with father, but they had a way of common understanding. Father's funeral was held at this Kobudera, and this old priest came from the Asakusa head temple to officiate at the ceremony. His presence on such an occasion was a source of great happiness for such a sentimental timid little fellow as myself. Of the many mourners that day, I was the first to offer incense before my father; as many eyes were riveted on me, with a mingled feeling of sadness and loneliness I performed the act. However, the thought of that saintly, kind priest standing just behind me, in his gold brocade and cape, who but a few years ago had patted me on the head and given me cakes, watching me with that same serene merciful expression, gave me such strength. I felt as if I had come there, after a long absence, to visit the temple again with my father.

Father was always earnest. Seated at his desk, he would work away at his manuscript, with his single very near-sighted eye, head twisted to one side, moving his scratchy pen rapidly. I can always see him in my mind's eye in this position in his study; it is one of my most sacred memories of him. When father was at work, his ear was deaf to all sounds; he never heard the voices near him. The oil lamp on his desk, the wick of which had been turned up too high, would be found to be smoking and the soot covering everything in the room by midnight. Sometimes, after he had crawled out of his mosquito net to sit at his desk the next morning, we would find under his desk many mosquitoes, rolling fat, like little red beans. Discovering them, mother and I would point and say to him, 'It must have been very itchy'; to which he would reply, 'I didn't know anything about them,' and he seemed surprised on further examination to find red spots in patches like the milky way, covering both his right and left legs. He was that much absorbed when at work.

On the other hand, in order not to disturb him at his writing, mother endeavoured to keep us

HEARN'S SELF-
PORTRAIT

KAZUO SWIMMING

A VIEW OF YAIDZU BAY

PEN-SKETCHES BY LAFCADIO HEARN

children away from him, and not make any noise.
It was his habit before sitting down to work, or
in the midst of composition, to walk up and down
the hall or in his study, thinking or trying to get
inspiration. While engaged thus, sometimes failing
to hit upon a good idea because of some unpleasant
family happenings or some outside annoyance, his
feelings got the better of him. Then he seemed to
be possessed of some evil spirit and would cry out.
Mother and I would be frightened and rush to him,
calling, 'Papa! Papa!' And our cries seemed to
call him back from this sort of nightmare. Then
he would scratch or rub his head and apologize,
'Pardon, pardon.'

While at Tomihisacho and teaching at the
Imperial University, father wrote his 'Far East'
and 'Kotto,' and completed six volumes. In the
mornings and evenings, I was taught English
reading and writing, and if the weather was good,
was later taken for a walk. At this place my next
brother Iwao and third brother Kiyoshi were
born. Father was very fond of Kobudera, so he
asked Ichirō Hori, a young man from Izumo, who
was an assistant at Egi Photographers, to take
various views of the temple gate, and *onigawara*
(its corner tiles with demon faces) which had been
handed down from the Kanei period (about
three hundred years ago), the old tombs and
other things, and father made use of them in his
book 'Exotics and Retrospectives.'

Mr. Hori later went to America and stayed a long time in New York. He returned a few years ago and held a photographic exhibition at the Mitsukoshi Department Store, showing all his own products. He is one of our first-class artists now, but in Meiji 30 (1897), he was only a rattle-headed young fellow, who used to come to our house bringing cards with pictures of geishas and artists or foreign women he had collected from tobacco boxes. At that time he was a great stammerer, but took delight in singing the popular song of the time on the names of various tobaccoes, 'Pinhead, Sunrise, Old, Cameo,' etc., which he sang in his clear voice. He would take me for a walk sometimes to Yotsuya, (next town to Ushi-gomé) and on one occasion treated me to *okame-soba* (some kind of noodles). He was the one to introduce me to this epicurean dish for the first time. He was frequently scolded by father — but I will tell more about that in connection with Yaizu seashore.

While at Tomihisachō (I believe it was autumn), grandfather used to have his stomach upset frequently. Father told him that this was due to his lack of exercise, so going to the field at the back of our house, he would practise archery. This was quite suited to the feeble condition of his body. At that time he would shut himself in his *inkyo beya* (retired person's room) and devote his time earnestly to repairing the arrow wings,

strings, or targets. Simply to watch him making
the targets was very interesting. He would paste
strong Japanese paper on wooden frames, like
drums. After sprinkling water on them, he would
dry them over the brazier. Struck with the end
of the finger, they would produce a drumlike sound.
On these he made bull's-eyes with Japanese ink.
Without being asked, I would sit by and try to
prepare the Japanese ink, in readiness for his use,
but in the attempt soiled my hands and the
matting, so I was more of a nuisance than help.
Grandfather would place these targets on the
cliff at the side of Kobudera, and from some distance, with one shoulder bare of sleeve, the old
man would take aim and let fly his arrow. He
nearly always hit the mark.

Our student Niimi and rickshaw-man Nakamura
frequently borrowed grandfather's bow and arrows
to try their hands at it, but their arrows would
fly in a curve or sway to one side or scrape the
ground on the way. They rarely if ever hit the
target. At these times father was usually a silent
observer, but on one or two occasions grandfather
taught him how to stand in position; at what
angle to raise his elbow, and how to draw the bow.
Then father, who never used eyeglasses, would
take a powerful lens, looking through it to make
sure of the direction; then putting away the glass,
he would take aim and hastily let fly the arrow.
Very strange to say, it would go straight and drop

near the target. Grandfather used to marvel at this feat.

After the arrows were shot, it was my delight to run and pick them up. Watching grandfather taking his slow, deliberate aim was a very tedious thing for me, so I would look up to him and shout, 'Hurry! Hurry!' One day, as grandfather was aiming with his last arrow, I was too impatient, and started out running to pick up the arrow before it was let loose, and I had hardly gone more than five or six feet when whiz it went close over my head, lifting my hair. At the same time frightened cries arose from the crowd behind; voices could be heard exclaiming, 'Ah! *abunai!*' (dangerous). They may have been the voices of father and grandfather. They were much frightened. The faces of the people standing at the back turned pale. After that, grandfather hid his bow and arrows and would never touch them again. Father said if the arrow had been just one inch lower, Kazuo would have been killed. To recall that incident, he said, made him feel as if he were hugging a piece of ice.

The children of the neighbourhood used to gather at Tomihisacho, if the weather was fine. At New Year's time the sky overhead would be covered with all sorts of kites. On hot summer days it would be filled with butterfly nets and long poles, tipped with sticky matter, for catching dragonflies, grasshoppers, etc. On other occasions it would be filled with gay laughter of children playing soldiers, tag, hide-and-seek, and other innocent games. Usually this laughter was not very noisy, but if too boisterous, our student would come out and ask the children to move farther away, and they would obey very quietly and go over on to Kobudera hill. Father, who was occupied in writing upstairs, was not disturbed much, but sometimes strange voices were heard, and it was found to be a team of pimply-faced lads come to play baseball. These fellows were sure to send their balls banging against our fence once or twice during their game. When requested to move farther out by our student, they would take no heed of his words, and the banging would be repeated.

At such times father, whose spirit was musing with the ghosts and goblins or communing with those of the other world, would suddenly be called back to the realities of this chaotic world again, on hearing the bang, and would cry out as if in pain. The student would go to the boys and repeatedly ask them to cease their noise, but this only increased their spite, and some of them would shout back, 'Bismarck said, a bullet has no soul!' When these baseball crowds came while father was out, my people took no heed of them. Grandfather, with his arms folded, used to watch their games by the hour, saying, 'They are great! They will become Masters of Arts! They will make fine

soldiers! They can strike the enemies' cannons
and strike back at them, or with steel gloves catch
the enemies' balls and pitch them back!' He
seemed to be impressed by their energy, but when
the ball missed and banged on our fence again and
again, he would say, 'Ah, poor! poor! You can't
go to battle at that rate!' So shouting out, he
would break into a hearty laugh. Later, we asked
our landlord to put up a board sign forbidding
ball-playing on the premises.

One of these teams was made up of boys of
refined appearance. They were always quiet. One
group, we learned, were Peers' School boys, which
our student discovered from the marks on their
caps. Nakamura, our rickshaw-man, said that
they were composed mostly of brothers or cousins.
The children of Dr. K., doctor of children and a
physician of the Imperial Household Department,
were among them. They lived in Yotsuya, we
learned, and the father was said to be one of the
best pediatricians of the district. A short time
after this, my younger brother had severe ague,
and this Dr. K. was called in. Of course he was
not the kind to be called upon so easily, so at first
he sent a young doctor, who was all politeness,
delicate and gentle in movement. Someone in our
family nicknamed him 'polite-language-flowing
doctor.' The second time the senior doctor came.
At that time father was sitting by the bed and
met the doctor. The old doctor, noticing that

father was a foreigner, began to put queries to him. 'What is your country? You may be a Japanese now, but what is your native place? Ah, so! Have you friends? Not many? Is that so, that's too bad. It must be lonely, isn't it? Where are you employed? Where? Imperial University? Oh, then you know Beltz or Schreiber or Schrippa. Um. They are all my friends.' Thus he spoke for some time, and his haughty language and manners are still stamped clearly on my mind. I was only seven or eight years old at that time, but his rude manner of addressing me made me quite angry. 'Are all these your boys? They are fine boys.' So saying he stared at us. In my experience I had never heard anyone but the low-class people speak to father, saying, 'Ya! Ijin.' But this grey-headed old man was an exception in his rudeness. Of course father and mother felt very uncomfortable and never called him again.

I remember, when I was about seven or eight years old, we used to play soldiers. Since the Triple Intervention (R.G.F.), all the Japanese began to think that it was inevitable that sooner or later we must fight Russia, and the children's games began to take their turn in this direction. As we played, we pretended that our foes were the Russians.

My brothers and I had father buy us small sabres that we hung from our waists, and we loved to hear them rattle. In our play I was always

made their proud leader. Once in a while we got
so excited over our battle that the two sides got
into a real fight. Many children were made to cry
as the result of our swords. The children would
come after me to play, and when I asked them to
play war, they would say, 'We like to play battle
with you, but you soon get too excited, so we
don't like to.' Did this come from two or three
timid fellows? No, it came from the lips of level-
headed lads, and I, who had the habit of flushing
easily, always kept aloof from them politely.

One day I was playing outside near our gate with
four or five of the neighbours' boys, with my
precious sabre dangling at my side, though we
were not playing war. A fellow wearing a striped
Japanese *happi* coat with black collar band and
chest protector, hunting cap on his head, eyes
drawn at the corners, yellow complexioned, came
near us. 'Oi [say], your sword is fine, isn't it?
Even if it were melted, the metal alone would be
quite valuable. Just let me look at it,' he said.
'No, I won't! You just look at it from where you
are,' I said. 'Where is your house?' he continued.
Just then Seikō Nakamura (our rickshaw-man's
son) pointed to the black gate and said, 'His
house is here.' The fellow went on, 'What's your
name?' I thought him a suspicious-looking fellow,
so I replied, 'Don't know; go away or I'll cut you
with my sword!' at the same time putting my
hand on the handle simply to show off my bravery

to my companions. 'Oh, I'm afraid! Good-bye';
and he left us.

In about five minutes he returned again, saying,
'I'm sorry for what I said a while ago. You don't
mind it?' So saying he gave me a green painted
stick about two *shaku* (about two feet) long. The
children all cried out for me to give it to them.
The hunting-cap fellow took advantage of the
situation and said, 'Say, if you fellows all want
such sticks, there's a place I know where I can
take you. There are lots of them that can be made
into canes for grown folks.' We children were
taken in by his smooth talk. 'Where? Is it far?'
all exclaimed at once. 'Botchan, come along, it's
just over there. If you get tired, I can carry you
on my back, like a general's horse; run around
with you, if you like.' The other children urged
me, so like a little fool, I was influenced by their
persuasions — and was led away by the cunning
youth.

He led us to a low land between Ichigaya Prison
and Kobudera. There the grass was higher than
our heads. He suddenly acted very strangely and
came suddenly to a halt — 'This is very near to
the prison, so you must not speak very loud. It's
not good to carry any cutting thing as tools or
sticks, for if you are caught, it is dangerous. If
we are caught here with a sword like Botchan's,
they will surely take it away from him,' gazing at
my sword while saying this. 'Then what shall we

do?' asked one of the children, and he said, 'Take it off and hide it in the grass — I will remember where you put it so it will be safe — then, after we have cut the sticks, get it again. It's all right, isn't it?' 'No, I will go home.' When I answered thus, he became excited. 'It's dangerous — you can't go home alone. Inside this grass, you'll get lost,' and so he stopped me. To be sure, to get here was no great distance, but he had led us in a very roundabout way. 'But I don't want to take off my sword.' When I insisted thus, he said, 'Then, Botchan, hide the blade only and you can carry the sheath. Then, if you are caught, you will be safe.' At this I yielded and drew out the sword from the sheath and handed it to him. He said, 'Botchan, it's here, remember. Oi, every-body, remember it's here!' So saying he stuck the sword among the roots of the small bamboo. 'Now, let's go to get the bamboo for sticks.' He led us into the thick underbrush, but there were no bamboos to be found large enough for making sticks. 'I'll go alone and try to find a good place and you wait here'; at which he left us and dis-appeared. After five or six minutes he came back, 'Oi! Oi! it was foolish. The bamboo, which I thought was here, has been cut down by the prison people. There isn't a single one to be found. Ex-cuse me, all. It can't be helped. Let's go back. Instead, I'll buy you all some *teppodama*' (or bullets, drop-candy). He led the way out of the

brush. Suddenly he stopped at the place where
my sword had been hidden among the roots of the
young bamboo, crying anxiously, 'It's gone! The
sword is gone! I wonder if the prison warden has
been here and taken it. Say, you all look around!'
At the same time he was pretending to look earnestly. The children and I hunted among the young
bamboo, but no sword was to be found. He began
to apologize, saying 'Botchan, *gomenyo* [excuse
me]! Botchan, *gomenyo!*' repeatedly.

With a mingled feeling of loneliness and sadness,
I became very unhappy, for I had been forbidden
ever to go outside of our back field without permission, according to father's instruction, and I
had disobeyed. I regretted it very much now.
That sword which father had bought for me —
which everyone had praised — that precious sword,
which had hung at my side but a few moments
ago, shining, of exquisite workmanship, beautifully
carved hilt, of gold arabesque, with pearl-like
beaded shagreen handle, from which hung a heavy
gilded tassel — to think of it! Something seemed
to stick in my throat. My eyes began to burn, but
I tried to hold back the tears. The young rascal
continued, 'Botchan, you lost the sword, so you
don't need the sheath any more; won't you give it
to me?' 'No, if I lost the sword, the sheath is all
the more precious to me,' I said. 'Um, that's so.
I'll try hard from now to find it for you, so don't
you worry. It's best not to tell anyone about it.'

He saw us all out to the path, then rushed back among the underbrush.

Sheath, without a blade, bladeless sheath, hanging from my waist! The children all gathered together complaining about the rascal taking us to a place where there was no bamboo, and then to offer to buy us some drop-candy. Such a liar! Thus complaining, we came home. Just as we reached our gate, Oroku, seeing my pale face, exclaimed, 'Botchan, is something the matter with you?' My heart was already full with my grief, so I could not reply at once, and Seikō burst out, 'He had his sword stolen!' '*Mah!* [why] Is it true?' she inquired. Then something which had been stuck in my throat seemed suddenly to burst, and burning tears began to stream down my face and soaked Oroku's apron. This took place just outside of our gate, so mothers and children of the neighbourhood gathered and began to inquire about the rascal's whereabouts. We foolish youngsters were led away, but Kenchan, whom we met and asked to join us, would not come. He was too wise. None knew where the rascal had come from. But Kenchan did. He knew. It was the tinsmith's errand-boy of Yotsuya.

So our students Niimi and Aki took Kenchan to see the boy. Tall Niimi, with his closely shaved head, and fat, bushy-headed Aki, with pouch-headed Kenchan as guide, presented themselves before the tinsmith's shop. Just as they appeared, the rascal rushed and hid the sword blade under a *happi* coat. He was wandering about on the floor in the front part of the shop. He was told to return the article under the *happi* coat or else come along to the police station. By the time we had got back my sword, it was already dark. With great relief, but much ashamed, I saw, by the dim light of the lamp, my sword safely returned to me, but the beautiful blade was soiled by hand-marks. We listened to what Niimi and Aki had to say about getting back the sword. 'I didn't take it. I found it in the bush,' said the rascal. 'Your thievish nature is not cured yet!' So saying, the boss slapped him in the presence of all who stood in front of the shop.

I was ashamed for a long time to tell my people and neighbours about this matter. Father said, 'Children who disobey their parents suffer such results. Don't have such an unpleasant experience again! In your after years, there will be a thousand kinds of tempters waiting to rob you. As you grow, be very cautious of such.' The next day, father made me read Mary Howitt's poem, 'The Spider and the Fly.' In this poem the foolish fly was lured by the flattering words of the cruel spider and was led to its web and eaten up.

Father finally became disgusted with Tomihi-sacho. One of the chief reasons was that the new head priest of Kobudera had all the fine old trees cut down and sold them to get money. Father had

become very much attached to these great old
giants on the hill and they were his friends that
greeted him mornings and evenings in his walks.
The water main was being laid and the streets were
all torn up with the digging, and the upheaval
in front of our house seemed to have no ending.
This was another cause of his dislike of this part
of the city.

Then, with the extension of the prison quarters,
the red-uniformed prisoners were marched in line
every morning and evening to work on the extended ground and frequently made their escape.

One evening, while father was walking up and
down the hall with a cigar in his mouth, suddenly
he heard someone running in the yard as if in bare
feet. 'Who is that?' he called out, but no one in our
house had gone out. The next morning a mark
was discovered on the fence where someone had
scaled it.

One morning, two or three years after the experience of my stolen sword, Itchan and I were in
front of Kobudera gate collecting some moss for
making a miniature garden. We saw something
coming down the stone steps lightly rattling a
chain. 'Ah,' we thought, 'a dog is coming down,'
and with no other thought we turned in that
direction. What was our surprise to see a fellow
in striped kimono with a grey coat tucked up,
wearing black gaiters, without *tabi* (the digitated
socks), sandals or other footwear. Barefooted,

hatless, tiptoeing his way, he rushed out from the
temple grounds, looking anxiously at us from the
high embankment. Hastily pulling his handcuffed
arm into his sleeve (from the opening of which the
chain was hanging visibly), he called out, 'Oi, good
children, if the police or someone comes this way
and asks if you have seen anyone, say that you
don't know.' So saying, glancing around with a
pitiable expression on his face, he jumped into the
bamboo grove to the left and disappeared.

Those slanting eyes — that yellow complexion
— I had a recollection of having seen them somewhere. 'Oh, it's him!' I exclaimed, after a moment.
Then Itchan also said about the same time, 'Sabre,
eh?' 'Yes,' I said. Not until a few years ago did I
tell of this to my people or the police. I never
wanted to tell it to anyone, especially to father, for
when the sword was returned to me, father said,
'But Kazuo, let us forgive that boy. Now let us
ask God to make him turn over a new leaf from
tomorrow.'

Father would get the barber to clip my hair, but
he would never allow the razor to touch my face.
My rosy, smooth, peachlike-skinned face he loved
to pat and kiss. He did not take much heed of
bruises on my hands or feet, but if there was the
least thing the matter with my face, he would be
very anxious. His expression at such a time was
that of pain — or sorrow would be nearer. In

spite of his warnings and care, however, I received frequent injuries during the skirmishes in our battle or robbery plays. These scratches and bruises were the results of my unthinking retaliation, for when I received a hit I would get very angry and lose my head. So my opponents, if they discovered that I was hurt, would always take to their heels.

Once during our play at battle, Seikō stabbed me from behind. 'What!' I exclaimed, and turning quickly about struck his bamboo spear with my sword; the bamboo flew and struck my face, leaving a few bruises. When Seikō saw this, he exclaimed, 'I give up!' and dropped his weapon. Our opponents shouted, 'The enemy leader is wounded!' and ran away as fast as they could. That evening at supper (though I tried to avoid turning my face in father's direction) father noticed the bruises, and said, 'Hereafter, when you play outside, I shall have Niimi or Aki to watch you.'

Niimi was very conscientious and always tried to follow father's instructions. He urged me to practise mechanical gymnastics or swings, etc., and tried to dissuade me from playing at battle, which was dangerous; but Aki was not so careful or severe. When he was overseeing us, we got hurt just the same. It made no difference whether this official guardian was near us or not. Finally he fell in with us and became the leader of one side. Again I received a crescent-shaped cut on my left

cheek, near the ear. While pursuing my enemy up
the slope of Kobudera, I stumbled against a post
without seeing it. This wound was not very con-
spicuous from the front, so I tried to avoid my
father's discovering it. But in the evening, when
I went to say, 'Papa, goodnight!' as usual, he laid
down his pen, raised my chin with his hand to kiss
me, when lo, the light from the lamp showed up
my wound in full view. Father was very much
frightened. 'When and where did you get hurt?
Wasn't Niimi or Aki near you?' So saying he went
down to the students' room with an angry expression on his face, and going up suddenly to Aki, who
was seated in front of his desk, shook him by the
shoulder. Aki turned in surprise and I heard father
exclaim, 'Careless! Irresponsible!' These were
simple words, but very cutting — and he was
scolded. I felt very sorry for him and did not
know what to do.

Years earlier my grandmother, while carrying
me on her back, had slipped and stumbled on the
steps of Nankōsha. In falling, she tried not to hurt
her grandson on her back, so did not loose her
hands from holding me, thus sustaining a great
wound, the scar of which she carried all the rest of
her life on her right cheek. Grandmother's
thoughtful self-sacrifice greatly impressed father,
but he was very sorry for her. In the years that
followed, whenever I was naughty and father
heard me talking back to her, he would always

say, 'Have you forgotten why that scar is on grandmother's cheek?'

Domestic dramas or historical plays showing beautiful personal feelings — or moralizing dramas — may be shown Kazuo, but never cruel, indecent, and base plays. Also, nothing below third-class actors. At this time Danjūro and Kikugōro, famous actors, were on the stage, and even though I was but a child and could not understand them, father thought it worth while to show them to me. For, as he said, 'True drama contains something which makes a deep impression on everyone — even a child — which will very often be recalled with pleasure in after years. Danjūro and Kikugōro are both old, so see them all you can before they die,' he always said to mother. For this reason I was taken to almost every performance of these great actors.

Theatres never had any attractions for father. He was always very busy writing and had no time to spare for such pleasures. When he began to write plays, the time might come when he would go to see them, he said. Father, while he was in America and acting as a newspaper-man, went frequently to the theatres, I was told. He went to interview famous French and English actors in their dressing-rooms very often. Some famous actresses were so proud that they would not permit reporters to interview them, but to father, they

were very good and met him politely, gave him
good materials, and showed him everything they
had, which they refused other men. 'It's strange,'
people would say, 'how that deformed fellow can
get into their favours.' They would envy and tease
him about it. 'Everybody became very jealous
of me,' he used to remark to mother.

Here is something quite different. It was once
when father went to see a movie. One evening
Lieutenant Fujisaki came saying that he was going
to Kanda Kinkikan to see the moving pictures and
couldn't Kazuo go. That day not only I, but father
and mother joined him. We were all seated on the
right-hand side upstairs. The performance started
with a phonograph which had a megaphone attachment. This was rolled to the centre of the
stage and Japanese records were put on. After this
was a sword dance by boys between twelve and
thirteen, and at last, the long anticipated pictures
came on. The first was of swimming and diving
from high stands. The next picture was the one
that we wanted to see — the English Transvaal
War picture, but it turned out to be a very repulsive and tasteless coloured picture. The colour
spoilt the faces and hands of the actors — made
them look dark, and their clothes and hats of dark
red, blue, or green seemed raised. When the mine
(which was purple) was about to explode, the
smoke effect looked like cheap painted papers
pasted on. Lieutenant Fujisaki said the military

march and camp appeared natural, but the picture of the combat and explosion was a trick which could be distinctly seen. The last picture was one of the President of the United States coming to San Francisco. This was colourless and natural, but the film was very poor and old, the spots marred the picture, and we seemed to be looking through hard rain or snow, and very indistinctly the people and vehicles passed before us with such speed that it quite surprised us. They no sooner appeared from the left than they vanished as quickly to the right. Father, although he put his glass to his eye and tried to take them in, could not get any good idea of them. We all took away very strange impressions.

I saw many good plays. Many people who go to theatres like to imitate the actors' manner of speaking, etc. (lately we have seen people imitating the ways and walks of American actors when on Ginza, taking long strides, squaring and raising one shoulder to appear like brave men). But to such a cowardly creature as I, the way the ruffian acted or some actor performed his part on certain occasions was all clearly in my mind — but to tell the story about it was beyond my power. On this point mother frequently said, 'This child has seen many famous plays, but I wonder if he understands them.' One day father took me for a walk and on the way told me two or three stories in connection with painting. Replying to him unconsciously,

I told about the stammering 'Matahei' very minutely. After returning home, father said, 'Kazuo is a great observer,' and related to mother what I had said. 'Then it was not useless to show them to him, was it?' she said.

In the days before there were trams or automobiles, when one went to the theatre there was a long line of rickshaws. We had to go first to the tea-house, then, after a formal rest, we passed through a board hallway, led by the tea-house guide, to our places in the theatre. The performance began at ten o'clock in the morning and lasted until eleven o'clock at night. During this long interval we were packed in a very small square enclosure, with just room enough to sit. Here we ate cakes, drank tea, sushi, fruit, etc., while looking on at the plays. In those days the intermission seemed to be very long; especially in Kikugōro's performances, they seemed longer. Mother used to get ready for theatre-going two or three days ahead — thinking about her hairdressing and clothes. On the day of going she would be very much excited; while at the theatre she seemed to be enjoying herself, weeping or laughing as the occasion called, but the next day she would be all used up and had to rest for several days on account of fatigue. 'Theatre is all right, but you will injure your health,' father would warn her.

At Ushigomé, father had many callers, but

when he was occupied in his writing, he disliked
to be disturbed, so declined to see visitors. Should
the caller happen to be one of his old pupils, he
would stop his work and see him. Father disliked
lies under any circumstances, so he instructed his
doorkeeper that should callers come, he should
tell them his master was very busy in his study and
ask them to state the nature of their business, but
never to dismiss them by saying that his master
was out. So many times, when callers came, the
doorkeeper was at his wits' end how to get rid of
them. Very often he was caught in the act of dis-
missing a guest with a lie, and on such occasions,
father would scold him severely.

The callers that father would always receive
were University students, Matsué Middle School
students, and Kumamoto High School day pupils.
I believe these people would like to say that, as
they had made contribution of materials for his
writings, they helped to make Hearn great. But
father was the kind that liked to gather his materials from any source. As young as I was, I can
remember that those who brought materials to
him were many—maids, servants, shopmen, work-
men, rickshaw-men, pilgrims, natto-sellers, street
singers.

Some of the stories brought to him for criticism
were scrappy, some repeated themselves, others
lacked a beginning or an end, some were bad.
These he would rewrite, enlarging sometimes,

omitting or correcting — arranging them properly, putting them into beautiful English — not even mentioning his part of the work, but always grateful to the originator of the story.

Father was always very grateful to Mr. Chamberlain and Mr. Amenomori, for from them he gained much help, it was said. But at that time I was only a child, so knew nothing aside from what I drew from their conversation.

Our distant relatives liked to come and make our Ushigomé house a free stopping-place whenever they came sight-seeing or job-hunting, as it was very convenient. These people father treated very kindly, if they were relatives who had been kind to mother when she was a girl (and the people into whose house she was adopted were always kind). These were always welcome, but the others were turned out. In Kumamoto there was a nephew of grandmother's, Nobu by name. This youth came and lived with us for several months. Afterwards, quite unknown to everyone, he passed the examination for the police service. Mother and grandmother denounced him for this secrecy, but father said, 'No, no, don't get so angry,' and tried to calm them. Japanese policemen he believed to be the most honest, good people in the world. But once he went to see the Bon-odori on purpose to see what it was like. The police of the place were haughty and rough in handling the merry crowd

and made them stop their dance. 'What a foolish
police!' he remarked. It was a great disappoint-
ment to him.

Nobu-san frequently came in his uniform. He
carried a police whistle on a black tasselled cord,
and I as a youngster would enjoy taking it out of
his pocket and blowing it loudly. 'Don't blow so
loud,' he would say, greatly troubled. He passed
the rest of his days as a policeman and advanced to
quite a high position of which he may well be proud.

While we were in Tomihisacho, mother's adopted
house relative by the name of Leitaro Takagi came
to visit us about three times. He was a saintly,
mystical man. He had travelled all over Japan, on
foot, I was told. His unshaven face was covered
with beard and his hair long — a very tall, thin,
fierce-looking man. He seldom opened his mouth
or laughed out loud, but when he did speak, his
voice was very gentle. He spoke carefully and
could tell long stories well. When he was quiet, he
would keep silent for two or three days without
uttering a word, simply pulling at his long whis-
kers. If mother or grandmother said anything
about his clothes, he seemed troubled. He did not
care to give them trouble in that respect. He only
wanted a place to stop and have his meals when in
Tōkyo, that was enough. And his meals, the
simpler the better. Costly gifts he refused. Father
called Takagi 'Long-legged man' and greatly respected him. Takagi was said to be able to see into

the future. Quite unlike many who claim such a gift, his sayings came true. It used to make us feel very queer. Once, at Matsué he said: 'Teacher [meaning father] is not one to remain here long. Presently, he will go to the south,' which afterwards turned out to be Kumamoto direction. He predicted from a long time ahead, the birth, sex, etc., of brothers and sisters, and his prediction was more true than that of the midwife. He could give personal advice about the future, the state of one's star, locate lost articles, without any mistake. Takagi's final prophecy about father was: 'Under a big rock is hidden a great treasure. Surely, some time it will appear on earth and draw the attention of the people, but that stone is in the way.' Then father said, 'If I die, that stone will move, but I should like to see the treasure before I die.' Takagi replied, 'Don't be in haste — don't be in haste'; but father said that he could not wait. To me he said, 'Botchan is very nervous, but you are aware of that, so it is nothing to worry over. However, all your life you will not be relieved of family troubles.'

This fierce-faced Takagi even patted me on the head and used to carry me on his shoulder like a horse or on his back or arm. He played with me with my building-blocks or balls and made snow-men in the yard. But even at these times, he did not show a smiling face. Takagi-san was taken with us to see the iris at Horikiri. I recall our tak-

ing him to Yokohama with us to call on Mr.
McDonald. He went walking many times with
father. Takagi-san was a kind man, but without
any previous warning, he would take leave of his
host and depart suddenly. He would come suddenly and leave suddenly — even in my childish
heart, I was sorry to have him go.

Another relative from mother's birthplace, Mr.
T. by name, came. No sooner was he presented to
father than he was scolded severely and had to
withdraw. This is why: father and mother, before
coming to Tōkyo, had taken advantage of their
vacation trip to Matsué to visit the grave of a certain relative. They went to the place in the cemetery where the grave was supposed to be, but look
as they would, there was no sign of a grave; the
ground of the spot where it was thought to be was
sunken in. They thought it very strange and went
to the temple office to inquire of the priest. 'Ah,
So-and-So's grave — that son of his sold it long
ago,' the priest said. Father and mother experienced very unpleasant feelings and returned to
their hotel. The cheeky Mr. T. who called at our
Ushigomé house was the rascal who had sold the
ancestral plot. 'Are you a son of a Samurai? Instead of selling and eating up your ancestor's
grave, why didn't you commit *harakiri* in front of
their tomb? Un-Japanese-like Japanese are not my
relatives. *Sayonara* [good-bye] — leave at once!'
Thus shouting, father flung into the garden the

partly smoked cigar that he had been smoking while sauntering in the hallway. Even now, I have a vivid remembrance of father's pale, angry face.

Oyasu-san, grandmother's niece by adoption, though beautiful, had a sad life. For some reason or other she had been married and separated several times. Takagi-san saw her and said: 'Oyasu-san is pretty, but there is a sad line of fate on her forehead. Ah, she will never be lucky. If that changes, it will turn into a dangerous weapon by and by, so be careful.'

Father said, 'If Oyasu-san has no place to go, let her stay. But as she is a woman who has changed husbands many times, though not unpleasant to look upon, still we have students in our house, and besides, other young fellows come to the house — we don't want any mishap — caution her about this. If she remains serious, it's all right to let her remain as long as she wishes, but people's tongues are troublesome and they will begin to say that Hearn has a concubine nowadays; so speak to her regarding her future and arrange for her to marry again and settle down.' In this way he warned mother. Oyasu-san left us after a month and returned safely to her native province. Afterward, she married and went to Manchuria, where she died.

Ichiro Hori, photographer, though not a relative, came to see father at Tomihisacho. He was an Izumo student. Teizaburo Ochiai, now a teacher

of the Peers' School, came to Tomihisacho house
two or three times. Mr. Ochiai never wore a college
cap, but always a hunting cap. To the doorkeeper
and the maids, he was very polite. Though he
came only a few times to our house, he left a very
good impression on us and the servants.

The Niimi brothers both lived with us. They
were of Shizuoka class (Samurai class), sons of
Masutomo Niimi, who had served for a long time
as an editor of the Yomiuri newspaper. The elder
brother, Sukeo, graduated from the Nautical
School and went on a training ship, the Tsuki-
shima-maru, which was sunk, and has never been
heard of since. Of the crew, only the corpse of the
captain and the mess-boy, with a few sticks of
wreckage from the boat, were found. We were all
surprised to hear this sad news.

Father, who loved the sea, experienced a great
shock at this accident. Some time later while
walking along the beach at Yaidzu, I picked up a
small white stone shaped like the head of a priest,
and when showing it to father he said, 'Isn't it
Niimi's bone?' in all seriousness. It was in reality
not a stone but a part of fish bone. Every time we
heard of a shipwreck after that, father seemed to
think of Sukeo. The younger brother Sukeyoshi
Niimi, was unlike his brother. He was more of a
man of talent — serious and steady. The elder
brother stayed with us only a year, but the younger
one remained three years. He went as far as Kōtō-

Gakkō (a high school), but owing to illness was obliged to stop. Father loved this honest youth. All Maruzen or Kelly and Walsh errands were done by him. Whatever errands father entrusted to him would be carried out to the letter, which pleased father so that at one time he gave the youth his own steel watch on the spot. Sukeyoshi had no sooner returned to his room than he hopped around in glee, putting the watch on his forehead, and surprising his companion. Whenever he was happy, he would cry out 'Yukai!' (Heavenly) in his comical voice. That was his habit of expressing happiness. But on this occasion, he hopped around the room at random like a grasshopper. He always accompanied father when he went for a walk or to Yaidzu for a swim. After father's death, he survived only few years and died at an early age.

To retire soon after supper was not good, father always said. So almost every evening after supper in the dining-room of twelve mats (which served also as the children's play-room), we all gathered, children, students, maids, and all, and sang songs. While singing war-songs, we would march around the large dining-table for about an hour. That became our custom. Father and mother sometimes joined us. On these occasions the time-keeper was the good-voiced Aki-san. Clumsy Niimi, whose Adam's apple seemed to trouble him in singing, would invariably get out of tune and

upset the harmony of this chorus. He was so un-
musical that father sometimes had to say, 'Niimi,
modulate your voice a little more!' *Kimigayo* (the
national anthem of Japan) and other songs —
Niimi sang them all to the same tune. Aki-san's
singing had rhythm and needed no criticism, yet
even he had mishaps occasionally. Once, because
he sang hymns too proudly, father called him
down — 'Don't sing songs in that way in my house.
It reminds me of the days when I was small, in my
school days. I can't tell you how unhappy it makes
me.' Another time young Aki-san was singing *La
Marseillaise* when father remarked, 'All French-
men would weep to hear such poor French,' at
which Aki-san was greatly disheartened. Sometimes, after moving the big table out of the way,
we would walk on the border of the mats singing,
'*Kompira, funé, funé*,' or play tag. In these games,
father frequently joined us. He learned most of
the war-songs that we children sang so he could
join with us. In '*Kompira, funé, funé*,' he was
specially good. But when father sang them, it
sounded like a child four or five years old singing,
in accent so innocent, so that if one heard him from
a distance, one would not imagine that it came
from the grey-haired old father — so cute and
baby-like his singing was.

Father always went to the University in the
rickshaw, but even in the summer he would not
permit the hood to be put on. With the exception

of vacation, every morning he left the house with a blue *tōchirimen furoshiki* (muslin wrapping cloth), containing a few books, tucked under his arm. As soon as he was seated, off would go Nakamura-jiiya with his swift feet. Summer or winter, it was just the same — his broad-brimmed grey hat on his head, from the edge of which curled up the smoke from his cigar, and with his parting words of 'Good-bye, darlings!' as he disappeared from the gate.

The rickshaw was his own, so it was kept in our yard. We had a man live at the house — later we hired the boss of the neighbouring rickshaw-house and Nakamura was the old man. 'Jiiya' (old man) had his own shop, but mornings and evenings he worked around the house like a regular house rickshaw-man. One day as he was pulling and running down a hill, near the crossing at the foot of the hill a bicycle suddenly came from the side. In trying to avoid collision, he quickly turned the shaft, when unfortunately one of the wheels went on the stone and before he could utter any warning, the rickshaw had overturned. '*Shimatta!* [My God!] Dropped my master! Bad-eyed master at that! Injured!' In an instant he uttered these words in his heart, anxiously extricating himself from under the shaft where he had fallen, and turned to find father gone. Before he could collect his thoughts, a gentle voice was heard saying, 'Are you hurt?' from one side. Father, with his glass in his right hand, holding to his one eye, was looking scrutinizingly at Jiiya's dust-covered body, pityingly, from head to foot. He came near and with the left hand brushed the dust off from his body. Jiiya was shrinking from him, but father did not in the least say any sarcastic words or scold him or argue. When father found that his rickshaw was going to turn, he jumped out to one side. Jiiya frequently recalled this incident, saying, 'With such a bad eye, he is so quick!'

Father's teaching hours, while at the Imperial University, were half a day, either in the mornings or afternoons. Except on Thursdays, when he worked all day, or when he was ill, he always took his lunch at home with his wife and children. On Thursdays, his time away from home was very long, so mother made this her going-out day. We mischievous children would exercise our freedom on that day. After father's return about four o'clock, we youngsters would go running and shouting up to him, hanging on both sides of him, trying to examine his pockets for goodies. His pockets would always contain oranges, pears, or other fruits or paper-wrapped cakes. These were souvenirs — desserts from Seiyōken which he had put into his pockets for us.

One night, under the yellow light of an oil lamp, with some water-colour paints from the Uyeno Exhibition, Niimi was drawing battleships, sol-

diers, horses, and all sorts of things for us. At the
time when mother bought the paint for us, she
strictly cautioned us never to put it in our mouths,
as it was poisonous. I was talking and singing while
Niimi painted, and became thirsty, so asked Oroku,
who was near, for a drink. Oroku brought some
warm water in a coffee cup and handed it to me,
saying, 'It's coffee,' and put it down at my left.
I thought it was really coffee. On my right was a
coffee cup too, just like it, which contained water
in which we washed our brushes. So the contents
now was the colour of coffee. Stupid me, looking
intently at the picture and not paying attention
to what I was doing, I carelessly took a gulp of it.
'This is bitter, there is no sugar.' At that moment Niimi exclaimed, 'Ah, it is different!' and
took it out of my hands. When I realized what I
had done, I thought to myself, 'Why, I drank
poison!' and thinking that I was going to die, I
cried out. That cry, even to myself, sounded
terribly; the whole house heard it and I was terri-
fied. Everyone came and gathered around me, asking, 'What is it? — What is it? —— ' Upstairs,
father, who had been writing, threw down his pen
and came down. Mother, who was taking a bath,
rushed out with only a towel wrapped around her.
Father said afterward that he thought I had overturned the lamp and got badly burnt, and mother
thought so too. When the truth was known,
mother scolded me, saying, 'What is it! — a boy

taking only a mouthful of paint water and setting
up such a howl!' So saying she reproachfully took
the paints and pictures Niimi had been painting
and tore them up, rumpled and stepped on them.
But as a result of this scene, I felt easy. 'Why,
only one mouthful of paint water and such a cry!'
— this was very strange to me. Up to this moment
I had been instructed that just to put it in the
mouth would kill me; but after taking the water, it
did not kill me — therefore, it has no bad effect
on life. This was the conclusion I came to. Father
reproached me as being a coward. 'You with your
ancestors who were not afraid to die, what do you
mean? Carelessness in little things may be the
cause of great results, as I have always said, and we
must always bear this in mind. Paint water is
poisonous, but fortunately you took only a little,
so it will not have any effect on your life. Don't
worry. But hereafter, always be careful.' So saying, he went upstairs. On his way out he whispered something to mother and mother said something to grandmother. Then I was given several
pills and, with grandmother, sent to take a bath.
My precious paints were destroyed, and I felt very
bad, but on the following Thursday, father had
mother and me join him at Uyeno Seiyōken during
his school intermission, and after lunch we went to
Uyeno Bazaar and there he bought me better
paints than before, carefully giving me special
directions about taking care of them. With these

paints father painted several pictures for me and
I made many also.

I painted a soldier on horseback, and thought it
a fine piece of work. I proudly showed it to mother,
and just as I had expected, she praised it, and even
said, 'You copied it, didn't you?' — but it really
was original. Mother's query made me think more
that it must be very fine. I showed it next to
father. He praised it too. The horse and soldier
were well painted, but there was one bad place —
mother and I looked carefully, but couldn't find it.
Then father said, 'The sword is hanging from the
right side, isn't it?' 'Yes,' I said, noticing the
error after it was pointed out to me, but it was
very regrettable at this juncture after I had worked
so hard on it. It really was very, very regrettable.
I felt as if something was sticking in my throat,
and my eyes began to burn, and then mother said,
'After having your mistake pointed out to you,
why do you weep?' Then she began to scold me.
Father said: 'I can sympathize with Kazuo's
regret. I know it well. You don't reproach papa,
I am sure, but reproach yourself. I understand
your present feelings. In reality, I have had many
such experiences up to now. I write, thinking
that it's all right and give it out, when those who
do not think well of me find something to criticise
in my writings. At such a time, I would think,
"There it is"; but it's too late. Kazuo's picture
critics were father and mother who love you. But

in the case of father, being in the book, it was the whole wide world. In such cases I thank my enemies and reproach myself. Thereafter, I tried not to make similar mistakes; I wrote to those who said bad things of me and thanked them. They have become my friends. Kazuo, I am sure, you will never make like mistakes in making such a picture. Oh, I am sure.' He uttered words of such meaning in his usual quiet way.

Birds and insects, whenever we caught them and showed them to father, he would always let free. One summer afternoon, with Niimi, Aki, and the neighbours' children, about ten or so, we went through the next field to Kobudera, each carrying lime-stick and butterfly nets, chasing dragon-flies, grasshoppers, and cicadas. By evening we had quite a number, and I proudly brought them home. Father just at this time was walking in the hall with a cigar in his mouth. I showed them to him. 'How interesting,' he said, pointing to their wings or breathing on them. As he realized that it was getting dark, he said: 'Before the sun goes down, let them out. These poor creatures otherwise would not know how to find a place to hide from their enemies.' Without observing the content any further, he hastily opened the cage and let them all go, saying, 'Good-bye, pass a fortunate day tomorrow.' He said that he would have liked to examine them more carefully before it got dark, but if they were kept overnight and they died, he would feel very sorry. He always cautioned us that in catching the cicadas, dragon-flies, etc., we must be very careful not to injure their delicate wings and legs, and to take very good care of them. 'Even flies; don't kill them in a cruel way,' he said. One day, while father was at work, a fly came and bothered him. It walked over his manuscript and troubled him in his writing, so he struck at it, then caught it gently between his palms, but it escaped between his fingers and came back again and lighted on his nose or wandered near the end of the pen-point. This time he caught it between his two hands and held it firmly, but while trying to take hold of it between his fingers, it escaped again. Regardless of this, it returned to bother him more. He was troubled to know how to dispose of it. 'No one that has had such luck in escaping death ought to be killed, not even a fly. It's a pity!' He caught it again, but, without pulling off its wings, he opened the window, and saying, '*Sayonara* [Good-bye], don't come again,' he let it go.

III

AT THE SEA

III

AT THE SEA

In the summer of 1897, with a view to locating a good swimming place, father went from Maisaka to Hamamatsu and then to Yaidzu, in Shizuoka Prefecture, southwest of Tōkyo. Here he got acquainted with Otokichi Yamaguchi for the first time. Father's friend, Mr. Toyohisa Tamura, formerly a teacher in Matsué Middle School, was at this time employed at the Hamamatsu Middle School, and through his persuasion went to Maisaka and Hamamatsu, but the sea at these places was too shallow and not fit for swimming, and so we left at once for Yaidzu. The sea here was deep and the waves rough. Father realized that he had found an ideal place and decided to remain here.

That summer we all set out in rickshaws, I sitting on father's lap, our rickshaw-men all in white coats and pants. Our rickshaws rolled along first through a tree-lined avenue, then between rice paddies, and over a long bridge, finally arriving at Maisaka. We stayed there only one night. The big hotel was full of people and the partitions between the rooms were only reed screens, so everything in the next room was in full view and a young child would soon get acquainted with the children of the next room. I thought it was interesting, but father did not, and he felt very uncomfortable.

Then at Yaidzu, first we stayed at Akizuki (Autumn Moon), a restaurant and hotel, for about a week. One night I woke up and heard people talking in loud voices. Something had happened. Hotel people came to apologize. At daylight my parents were still angry over something and left the hotel. I learned later that, about midnight, mother overheard people at the hotel counter saying, 'Squeeze all you can out of these foreigners and make them get out by the festival day — *Nah?*' She told father and he was so provoked that he called up the proprietor, settled the bill, and got out as fast as we could. They brought us a basket of fruits and bowed repeatedly in suave manner as if to apologize for what they had said.

Mr. Tamura's boarding-house was run by a woman, wife of a fisherman, but a sole proprietress and mother of five or six children — black, salty-looking urchins. With her as our guide, father, mother, and I left the unpleasant hotel and went to pleasant Otokichi Yamaguchi's place. Here we were settled and contented, though it was a low-ceilinged and flea-infested place. Otokichi and all Yaidzu people, male and female, spoke in loud voices — that was their nature — but the proprietress of Mr. Tamura's boarding-house was an exceptionally loud-voiced woman.

After this, almost every year in summer, we went to Otokichi Yamaguchi's house. There we were free from callers. No one knew where we were, and only the person who introduced us to the place, Mr. Tamura, and at that time a military cadet, Hachisaburo Fujisaki, and the photographer, I. Hori, came. The first year (1897) and the second time (1899), comical Tamura came almost every day. He played with me more than he visited father, it seemed to me. In his pleasure moments, father often told us goblin stories in his poor, ungrammatical Japanese, in a Japanese-like manner, the meaning of which we understood very clearly. Toward dusk, this big-eyed, big-nosed man looked scary as he related these tales, and his face even looked so pale that I would frequently cry out for him to stop.

One evening, we were all gathered together by the window upstairs, listening to father's story about the spirit of the Chinese Bell. On this occasion, Tamura was present. Father went on to say that every time this bell was struck it sounded sad, for as the bell was being cast, an innocent maiden jumped into the melting flame, and it was her

spirit wailing that gave the bell its sad tone. We
were all intently listening and some were even
shedding tears, when Tamura alone broke out in
laughter. 'It's not a laughing story!' father said
with serious face. Tamura held his stomach laughing. 'But it's funny.' He was shaking so he finally
rolled all around the floor struggling in such a
condition.

'Our soldier!' father called Mr. Fujisaki. He
called on us in the summer of 1897, and on his return home climbed Mount Fuji with father. We
saw father and Fujisaki start off on horseback and
I was envious of them. I remember saying, 'I'm
going to ride a horse when I become a man.'
Mother and I stopped at a hotel in front of Gotemba Station and passed two lonely tiresome
days. The time we waited for father seemed very
long. At this time it really did not seem as if it
were only two days — it seemed ages. I went out
a number of times a day into the back yard to look
up at Mount Fuji, thinking, 'Papa climbing it
now'; Mount Fuji stood at the back of the hotel —
not the white, grand, inspiring Fuji, nor green nor
blue, but a brown or reddish-coloured Fuji. It was
just the kind seen in Hokusai's picture.

Mother, who was young then, carrying my
younger brother and leading me by the hand, went
to the front of the hotel to welcome father back, as
he returned from the mountain climbing in the

conventional pilgrim's attire of big mushroom hat,
straw-matting cape, and a staff. We all laughed
heartily at this sight. Father's souvenirs were
nothing but sacred papers and lava and I was very
much disappointed. I made up my mind that that
staff was to be mine when I got home. Ten years
later, 1907, Mr. H. Fujisaki's father, a former
Major in the Army, G. Fujisaki by name, and I
climbed Fuji on horseback, starting from Gotemba.
It seemed a curious fate that just ten years ago, as
I recalled, my round-shouldered father and active,
ambitious, broad-chested H. Fujisaki, climbed from
this very place. The military cadet H. Fujisaki is
now an old colonel and is a grandfather of many
children. Young Kazuo is called Papa now; but
Mount Fuji, with its many climbers every summer, stands unchanged as of former days.

One afternoon, in the summer of 1900, Otokichi
called from downstairs that there was a guest from
Tōkyo. Hardly had he finished announcing when
we heard someone thumping up the stairs, making
a great noise like a jumping-jack. It was a man
dressed in a big checked foreign summer suit with
knee pants and red necktie, smelling strong of
highly scented perfumery, and a pale lavender
handkerchief sticking out of his breast pocket.
He was a photographer from Tōkyo. This fellow,
as I have said before, was a great stammerer, but
talkative and rattleheaded. 'Tu-tu-tu-two days,
I-I-I stay wi-wi-with you.' This was his initial

remark. Just at this time father was seated near
the window, writing to mother, and he was taken
by surprise. 'Ah, it's Hori, is it?' he said, smiling.
Hori came up to father and peeped at the letter
father was writing, 'O-oh, to your wi-i-fu-u.' Just
then father asked our student, 'Did you receive a
letter from Hori saying that he was coming?' The
student said 'No.' 'Then did a letter come from
home saying that Hori was coming?' To this the
reply was also 'No.' 'Then did Kazuo receive it?'
and I said 'No.' Then father said, 'I have not
received any letter from Hori-san or from home or
anywhere telling of his coming. Hori-san, who gave
you permission to come here? Did you come here
of your own accord?' Hori said 'Yes.' As he said
this, father turned directly to Hori-san and said,
'Then you are not my guest — you are a cheeky
thing — very rude — go back at once.' Hori ran
precipitately out of the house.

Yamaguchi Otokichi's house was open on the
east and west and closed on the north and south.
It was a two-storied, board-roof house, with three
rooms upstairs and three downstairs. Stones as
large as a man's head were used to keep the boards
from moving. In front was a fish shop and a big
tub over which was placed a chopping-board. The
tub contained red fishy-smelling water, and several
pieces of ice and dead fishes. In the room adjoining
this was a stand containing some lemonade bottles

and pears arranged in order. Under the eaves of
the house at the entrance were hung straw sandals
and dried fish. Near the entrance was a large pillar
which shone like bronze, and on it was hung a big
clock. At one side of this pillar was a 'Kamidana'
which in father's book is called 'Japanese Miscellany'; on it were placed many of Otokichi's
Darumas, some with eyes and others without eyes.
(The stairs were such that even a cat could not come
up without making a noise.) Father rented the
upstairs rooms for the whole of the summer. All
the rooms had low ceilings. The front room faced
the sea, but the houses opposite obstructed the
view so we could not see it. Even had there been
no houses, it would have been impossible for us to
see the sea, as there was a great dyke. From here
we got a strong smell of dried fish — the air was
full of it; we could see the sunburned, half-naked
people, young and old, men and women, and
indigo-coloured swallows glittering in the summer
sun as they flew about. Just opposite was a cake
shop, a tobacco shop, a liquor shop, and the boss
fisherman's house. From the back window upstairs we could see the side of a well, near which
grew some tall corn sunflowers, looking like the eye
of a great monster glaring at us. Beside these
there was a double go-down with white walls,
which glistened in the summer reflection, and in the
moss-covered old foundation of which crabs lived
and could be seen crawling in and out, here and

there. Behind the go-down was a small stream where ducks and drakes always swam.

Upstairs in every room, the lower part of the wall was pasted with old newspapers or Japanese colour prints. These papers were changed once in three years, if I remember correctly. Every time we went to Yaidzu, it had undergone some changes: first of all, inside the house the Darumas and various household articles, such as plates, etc. The most noticeable was the roof, which was changed before we knew it. The old boards had been changed to tile and the matting renewed. Out near the sea the dyke had been changed to re-enforced concrete and extended many *chō* beyond what it had been.

The babies of the neighbourhood seemed to have increased, but our old friends were all strong in this place, though, during the seven years we went there, I often heard of fishermen's boats having been wrecked. For a few days after we arrived, whenever father went to the sea or for a walk, many children followed us in procession, and Otokichi used to say, 'It's not a show!' Then with surprised expression father would look around and remark smilingly, 'My! what a number!' At one time he said, 'Yaidzu babies will soon fill all Japan.'

This place, now a very famous dried-fish (*katsuo-bushi*) manufacturing centre, thirty years ago was a very miserable little village. Unless one was curious, one would never take the trouble to go to such an out-of-the-way place. The city people or foreigners never came there, so for father it was a secluded place. At present Yaidzu has buses and taxis — a cinema hall too; but in the Yaidzu of those days, there were only doctors, travellers with heavy baggage or travelling actors advertising their faces, riding in rickshaws. Father warned me not to make fun of the village urchins, saying, 'If a quarrel takes place with these Yaidzu children, then the blame is on you. It will be because you have some unkind trait. Yaidzu children may be rough, but they are honest, no liars or mean ones. Show your warm heart toward them,' he strictly warned me. For this reason I was very careful and never quarrelled with the village children, and they were all my friends. Really, in Yaidzu there were no cowardly cry-babies as in Ushigomé and Tōkyo. There were no boys like 'Kaki-ko,' who, seeing father's face, would run off shouting something bad, or the cheap cake-shop boy 'Kin-kō,' who would wait at a distance for father to come out, and then shout something naughty in a comical voice. No such boys were found in this place.

At Yaidzu beach, seven or eight *ken* (forty or fifty feet) from the shore the water became suddenly deep, so that one could not stand up. This particularly pleased father. The beach was covered with large pebbles, so unless one went in quite far, there was no sand, but the water was very clear and the waves strong and high. Like distant thunder, it came rolling in, and this gave father great enjoyment.

To me, Otokichi Yamaguchi is a dear name. He was a thin man but strongly built, black, jolly, and good-natured. Healthy-looking, with no beard or moustache, he had a thin, long face with a wide space between his eyes, and eyebrows which had a comical slant, and with peculiar eyes. On the side of his nose, extending down toward his mouth, was a deep crease. Whenever he was asked anything, he always began his reply with 'Hé, hé-i ——' Father always said of him, 'An honest and fine fellow.' To the poor and rich, old or young, man or woman, to everyone, he was honest and greeted them with his 'Hé, hé-i.' It was a miracle how such a nervous man as father could put up with a place so full of flies, fleas, mosquitoes, bad smells from fish entrails and drying fish, poor ventilation, too bright sunshine, low-ceilinged upstairs rooms — all without a single word of complaint — and enjoy the place for over a month at a time, because of the genial Otokichi and his family and because of his love for the sea. Here he was not bothered by disagreeable visitors from Tōkyo or Yokohama. But the chief reason for his liking this place was, as already said above, Otokichi's character, which he admired. Father always called him 'Otokichi-sama' and Otokichi called father 'Sensei-sama.' Child as I was, it surprised me to hear father say, 'Otokichi-sama is like a god.'

Otokichi's wife was not so jolly as Otokichi —
as compared with him, she may be said to have
been too quiet, or one might say that she was so
cool-headed. Yet she was honest, too, and as a
wife and mother she was a firm character. For a
Yaidzu woman, she was fair, and her black hair
was curly at the ends. Like her husband, she spoke
frankly to father and she was a good *obasan*.
Between them the couple had two daughters and
a son. The youngest daughter Saki came to work
for us when she was thirteen years old. The first
two or three days after she came to our house, she
was so homesick that she used to go to the field at
the back or under the Kobudera gate to weep.
Later she became a very thoughtful and model
maid. She was the housemaid, and because she
was Otokichi's daughter, she was loved by father,
mother, and the rest of us, so later she became the
target of jealousy from other maids.

In the summer of 1898, father was persuaded by
Mr. Tamura to take the whole family to Sōshū,
Kugenuma, a seaside resort. We put up at the
Azumaya Hotel. The Billikins-like Tamura was
with us, and every day he did such comical things,
so that not only the hotel people but guests were
amused by his doings. He would go out in his
yukata on one occasion and again in only a *hanten*
— or sometimes in a woman's dress, or only with
a breechcloth and a towel tied around his head

like a coolie. Then again he would be wearing a nice silk summer *haori* over his naked body and his head tied up with a towel. These were his make-ups, and he used to parade the beach at Kugenuma — such a comical fellow he was! Tamura was a man who made his wife his inferior, so a question of divorce was brought up. Father wrote to him at the time, giving him good advice, and that letter was lent to me after father's death for publication along with various other letters of father's that I was collecting. When I asked Tamura for it, he said: 'As for myself, I feel ashamed to have that letter Mr. Hearn sent me regarding my divorce published. But it really shows his beautiful character, so even though you leave all the others out, I should like to have that one published. If I make my disgrace known by it, it's all right.' So saying, he lent it to me. He was a fine gentleman.

Father wanted to put me in the sea at Kugenuma, so he started out by teaching me to swim. But this place was different from Yaidzu, for there was no such good fellow as Otokichi to help us, so it was of no use. I always hung on to Mr. Tamura in order to be saved if father tried to take me into a deep place. Tamura would take me up on his shoulder and run off, shouting, '*Kora-sho, kora-sho!*' So, just as I had been about to become a swimmer at Yaidzu the previous year, here at Kugenuma, it was all undone, and I became timid and afraid of the sea. This was a great disappoint-

ment to father, and the sea here was too shallow
to suit him. Another objectionable feature was
that the hotel was always filled with guests from
Tōkyo and Yokohama, and very noisy, and father
did not like that. But this summer, grandfather,
grandmother, maid, student, and all were with us.
They took turns and came down, so for the sake of
the family, as father remarked, we stayed there
three weeks, swimming, picking up shells, catching
crabs, making sand mounds, etc., and happily
passed the time.

On father's desk there were always three or four
rare shells which we had picked up at Yaidzu, of
various shapes and colours. Father would stop in
the midst of his writing and look at these shells;
his thoughts were always with the sea and they
seemed to calm his feelings. Sometimes he would
pick up one of them and put it to his ear, saying
that he could hear the sound of the waves. Once
in a while he would put them to my ear, and ask,
'Can you hear the whisper of the ocean?' Father
wanted his children to know the sea well. To me
he used to say: 'Kazuo must learn about the sea
and become a friend of the sea. Kazuo knows the
fright of the sea, but Iwao does not,' he used to say
to mother and Otokichi when we were at Yaidzu.
Again, he would say: 'Kazuo is too much afraid of
the sea, but Iwao is not afraid of the sea. I must
teach Iwao the fearfulness and danger of the sea.'
And he tried to teach him, but it was quite useless.

Thankful to say, I got so that when I was thrown
into the sea, I could not be drowned; but instead of
making me love the sea, it made me guard against
it. As compared with me, my brother, even now,
has no fear of the sea. About ten years ago he was
carried into a deep whirlpool and almost drowned.

But when we went swimming together it was not
brother or I that gave father trouble, nor mother
or grandfather, but our maid, Oyone. She was
born in Izumo, and had come to work for us when
she was twenty years old. She was our kitchen
maid for a number of years. She married at thirty
and had one child, but unfortunately she lost her
husband and child, and afterward married again
twice. By her third marriage she had six children,
but they all died as well as her husband, so she
returned again to her former master. She was certainly an unfortunate woman. In appearance she
was a queer type, with protruding forehead, flat
nose, high, deep-set eye-sockets with very small
eyes, and thick, ugly lips. An anthropologist
would only have to look at her to pronounce her a
certain type of barbarian instead of pure Japanese.
Even father, who had travelled around the world
and had seen many types of features, used to say,
'What a strange head!' Looking intently at her,
'What a peculiar skull owner!'

At Kugenuma, one day, the old folks, children,
parents, and everyone went into the sea, hand in
hand. Oyone was with us. She could not swim at

all, but she broke away from us and kept going out farther and farther. Father saw her, and was very much frightened, so he went after her and took her hands. 'Danna-sama [master], the sea is interesting, isn't it?' So saying, she broke loose from father, going but deeper and deeper, to her breast, then to her shoulders. Here father forced her to stop. Afterward he said, 'I was about to commit double suicide with that foolish woman.' Then father told us of an experience he had in the West Indies. One day he was swimming side by side with a native, when suddenly the native disappeared. Soon afterward a big tail of a man-eating shark appeared. But this fright he got at Kugenuma was worse than that. Whenever we talked of Kugenuma, he would recall this experience with Oyone.

I was almost constantly with Tamura. He took us to Enoshima, and there bought me shells and toys of various kinds. Whenever father wanted some fire for the brazier, instead of ringing a bell or clapping his hands, he would blow a shell horn, which was one of the things father bought when he went with Tamura to Enoshima. He wanted something larger, but none of the stores had it at that time.

One day, Mr. McDonald and Mr. Amenomori came from Yokohama, and these two, one Eastern and one Western fat man, swam with father. Mr. Amenomori's crawl was quite different from Mr.

Tamura's dog style of swimming, and was very fine. Mr. McDonald was a trained swimmer, but neither of them could float so easily as father.

At the back of the hotel was a swing. Every evening I would get in it and be pushed by someone and took great pleasure in it. One evening, as usual, I was in the swing when father came and pushed me, and with two or three reckless strong pushings sent my small body way up, so that mother and grandparents, who were watching him, cried out, 'My, it's dangerous!' With every push father would puff his cigar and send the smoke into my neck, and would caution me not to let go my hold. 'Even if you swing off the seat of the swing, if you hold on tight, you will be all right. If you let go, you will get badly hurt.' In this way he would spur me on. At first I was afraid, so I held on tight to the rope and shouted for him to stop, but by and by it became very interesting and I got so that I would urge him to send me higher, and if someone else was pushing, I would ask him to do the same thing. Two or three times I slipped from the seat-board, but held on tight to the rope, so that I did not fall or receive any injury. I became more and more bold and became very fond of the swing, so after we got back to Tōkyo, father had a swing and gymnasium outfit put up in our garden.

While at Kugenuma, every evening father took a bottle of Japanese wine at supper-time: usually only one bottle. I felt envious of him and wanted

a bottle and small cup to drink from, so the maids
always put the same kind of bottle and cup on my
tray as father's, but filled with hot water. 'Papa's
wine is yellow, but mine is white,' I used to say.
Then they began to put tea in the bottle so as to
make the content look like father's. After that,
every evening the bottle and cup were put on my
tray. 'Botchan, let me pour out the wine,' said
the hotel maid. Like a grown person, I proudly
sipped the wine, to show off. In my remembrance,
it was only at Kugenuma and Yaidzu that father
drank Japanese wine, and only at night.

All the time he was in these bathing resorts, he
always wore Japanese clothes in the hotel or walking on the beach. In Tōkyo, when he was at home,
he always wore Japanese clothes, but when he went
out for a walk or to school, he wore foreign clothes.
His foreign clothes were only two kinds, winter and
summer. Summer ones were like those of the
policemen, made of white strong duck cloth, and
the winter ones were sober grey woollen cloth. His
hats were wide-brimmed felt winter ones, one grey
and one black, both the same shape, of very good
quality and expensive. The black one he seldom
wore. Frock coats and silk hats he disliked and
would not wear them, but mother had a tailor come
when at Kōbe, and had him make a frock-coat suit
after almost quarrelling with father. This was the
only suit of the kind he ever had. It was worn
on only two occasions — the Emperor's visit to the

University and the funeral of Dr. Toyama. Father never made a single New Year's call in Tōkyo.

Father's second and third toes overlapped and grew together. This was the result of wearing too small shoes in boyhood. For this reason he used to call very pointed shoes 'Barbarian footwear' and detested them. He always wore broad-toed, soldier-like shoes, even with a frock coat. Besides two pairs of these soldier's shoes, he had none other. Even for children he encouraged wearing clogs or sandals and avoided wearing shoes. His foot was very strong and he could walk easily two or three *ri*, but the sole of his foot was very much softer than ours, so he could not walk barefooted on the hot sand or pebbles on the seashore. At Yaidzu beach, where there was no sand, but only pebbles, it was very hard for him to walk any distance. Noticing this, Otokichi took some very soft rags and made father some sandals to wear whenever he went to the sea. Otokichi had them ready to hand out to father when going into the sea or coming out.

Father at Yaidzu laid aside his individuality and became like any ordinary person, wearing a *yukata* (summer dress) all day, and going out in *zōri* (straw sandals). Everywhere he was cheerfully greeted and he responded in the same manner, to young or old. Everyone addressed him as 'Sensei.' He jumped naked into the sea, and walked a great deal. He often walked to the shrine of Yamato-dake-no-mikoto, which was surrounded by green

rice stalks. We frequently went to where the black
dragon-flies played around Ogawa-no-Jizo near a
small stream, or along the breakwaters, welcomed
by the waves, passing along the pine avenue;
through reed-grown swamps by narrow paths
where red crabs played in numbers. We would
stop at Wada peninsula and rest at the tea-house
of a woman who had lost her son in the sea, and
drink lemonade.

In Tōkyo, father said life was too short, and
would send regrets to meetings and shut himself
up in his study, always with pen in hand. But
here he was really making it a rest time. Mornings
and evenings, he would devote to my lessons and,
instead of taking naps, he would read or write to
mother who was staying at home, sometimes drawing funny illustrated pictures in his Japanese
letter. Aside from this, he never took up his pen
or paper. If he saw something new or heard something of interest, he would jot it down in his note-
book in pencil for future use.

Father was very much interested in the Yaidzu
festival, especially in the children's dances. Each
section of the village contributed various kinds of
dashi ningyo (a festival car with image), and besides this, the Shintō priests passed in the procession on horseback, followed by a *miko*, a maiden
between twelve and thirteen years old. Then came
a fine-figured young man, half-naked, with a white
towel tied around his head, wearing white *tabi*

(digitated footwear), carrying a large branch of *sakaki* (a sacred tree). Each year the *miko* maiden and *sakaki* young man were selected from different people. This young man carrying his *sakaki* branch, surrounded by fifteen or sixteen stout-looking young men, also half-naked, stopped just in front of Otokichi's shop. At an order of 'Are you ready? One, two, three!' he raised the *sakaki* branch high over his head, and the young men who surrounded him rushed up from all directions trying to seize the *sakaki* branch. It was the duty of the young man to prevent them from getting the branch. This performance went on for about ten minutes. The confusion started at the turning of the village street and continued for two or three *ken*, and soon the *sakaki* branch was broken up. The people tried to pick up the broken pieces of the branch, leaves or bark; old, young, and children gathered there trying to pick up something, for if these bits were kept on one's person, it would bring one good luck and prevent illness for a year.

Among the young *sakaki* bearers this year was one young man, quite different from the others, strong and firm so that he was able to ward off the adversaries and pass the crowd without injuring even a leaf and go safely on, just as if the street were empty, till he finally reached a safe place. All, including father, exclaimed, 'My, what a strong man!' and marvelled at his coolness and strength. 'Kazuo, don't you want to be strong like

that?' he whispered in my ear. I replied, 'No!'
Father asked again, 'Don't you want to be like
that young man? Don't you like it? Do you
think it is hard?' I said: 'I should like to be strong
like that man, but I don't like that man in reality.
I do not like the fellow who does not even smile or
show his teeth, and such an unattractive fellow.'
I said this without hesitation. I disliked this wonderful strong fellow displaying his strength. Rather
than being impressed, I hated him. Father asked
why I hated him, and I replied, 'Because people
wanted the *sakaki* and he would not let them get a
single branch. He was only proud and puffed up';
and I showed father by puffing out my cheeks.
Father was greatly amused by this and laughed
heartily. 'If Kazuo was that strong young man,
what would you do?' he asked. 'I would do as they
did every year, after two or three rubbing up, I
would let them all take it.' 'That will not do, that
is cowardly. It is not mercy,' father said. 'That
young man has no one but himself to protect him,
and he has to fight the crowd as if they were his
enemy. His duty is to carry the *sakaki* branch
safely to the resting place on the seashore where
the *mikoshi* [portable shrine] is. That was his duty,
regardless of anything. To realize his duty — it
was heroic! From the ancient time one who was
heroic has been always without any amiability.
He did as he pleased and was not moved by others.
Amiable persons were scarce. Among the strong

there are always such stable persons. So if there is no man that much stronger than that *sakaki* man, they must all unite as in one strength to protect the branch. But in this case it is just that we should praise him, for he used his strength against so many,' father said.

At Yaidzu, father always took a walk at night. One moonlight night, Niimi and I were with him as usual. After walking for some time along the shore, we changed our direction and turned into a paddy-field path to Yaidzu Shrine. In the moonlight the mountains in the distance were clearly visible. The little frogs, frightened by the noise of our footsteps, jumped into the water of the paddy-fields. The air which entered our lungs seemed to penetrate to the bottom of our abdomens. We all three inhaled it as deeply as possible.

'The province of Suruga, oh, how beautiful! Niimi-san, your home was Suruga, wasn't it? Just over that mountain, isn't it? Suruga is a fine place.' When father made this remark, 'Yes, it's a nice place,' Niimi replied.

As we walked along, our shadows were very interesting. First of the three moving-figures and longest up to now, was Niimi's, which seemed now longer and longer on the ground. It seemed longer than the old shrine forest height beyond. 'Which do you like better, your birthplace or Tōkyo?' When asked this question by father, he replied:

'I love my birthplace much more, but for study, I think Tōkyo is a better place. At first, I hated Tōkyo — and even now, I dislike it a little.' Father, hearing this, was very glad. Niimi was of 'Shizoku' (or Samurai) family; this was his pride. This pride in his native place, whose ancestors' blood flowed through his veins, father did not blame it at all.

After we had been going to Yaidzu for but two or three years, we were once looking out of Oto-kichi's back window upstairs, to the west, where we could see green paddies and mountain chains, when our eyes caught sight of small toy-like trains about three *chō* [three or four hundred yards] away, which were running past frequently. We learned that they were carrying calcite or calc-spar. The cars were so small that I wanted to ride in them once to see how it felt. One day father, Niimi, and I were out walking, and on the way met this little train at the crossing. 'Shu-shu-shu!' the little engine sputtered. As it passed by, someone shouted from the engine, 'Ya, Niimi-kun, isn't it?' As I heard this, I looked up and saw at the pass-ing train window a face besmeared with oil, soot, and dirt, bushy-haired, and showing his teeth. 'Niimi, is that your friend?' father inquired, but Niimi was shaking his head and could not think who it was. Several days afterward, this small train engine had some boiler trouble and, for an unknown reason, burst. The engineer was covered by the steam and before the doctor could come, he died of burns. Two or three days after this, Niimi, looking over some old Shizuoka newspapers next door, learned for the first time that the dead engineer was a friend of his primary-school days. 'I thought it might have been he, but could not believe that he could be doing that kind of work — he was so dirty and black, so covered with hair all over his face. I can hardly believe that it could be he,' Niimi said, sadly. Father hearing this, gave Niimi one day's leave in order to go and pay respects to his dead friend.

After that, when I looked at the little train, it made me feel queer, and a hysterical voice seemed to come from the centre of the engine as if waiting for a chance to do some mischief. It seemed to wait patiently, this repulsive monster.

Niimi said that the dead engineer was a very good friend during their school days. Early in the morning before school they went together to the hills and picked strawberries or mulberries, staining their small lips reddish-blue. He at that time had a fine voice and used to love to sing, 'Kasumi-ka-kumo-ka...' (Mist or cloud or snow song). His voice sounded like a silver bell as he sang in the morning mist and it echoed from valley to valley. His school standing was said to be good, but he could not go to the higher school, as his people were poor. Niimi's family all came to the city, but his friend remained in their province.

Hearing this, father went on to say: 'I had a friend when I was young. Very jolly, frank boy. He had a fine voice and sang many sweet songs. He was always a kind and good friend, but at school he was rough and a leader of the youngsters. He was therefore scolded frequently by the teacher. He was spanked very often, but the teacher used to shake his own fingers afterward because they stung. The one who was spanked did not seem to be hurt and did not cry, but only smiled. His buttocks were so hard that the spankings did not make any impression on him. Later the teacher stopped using his own hand, but resorted to a whip. Even then the boy never cried, nor showed the least sign of being hurt. But he was not such a tough, savage boy as he seemed to be. He was a handsome youth with bushy golden hair, with red cheeks like an apple, and with big blue eyes. Later he entered a naval academy and became an officer, but died, strong boy though he was. This is how it happened: One day an untrained sailor fell from the boat. He could not swim, and the officer jumped into the sea after him. One who is about to drown will grasp at even a straw, and the sailor frantically grasped the officer. In the rough sea, with the big fellow clinging wildly to him, even the best of swimmers could not stand it. So while attempting to save one of his subordinates, he lost his own life. Kazuo reminds me of him somewhat. When Kazuo grows up, and should find it necessary to use a foreign name, then Leopold is a good name. It was the name of this friend. I always feel an attachment for it.'

Just as I was beginning to be a good swimmer, at the end of the summer of 1900, father one day said before we went to the sea, 'Today we are going to gain great advantage. You must do just exactly as I order you or you will be killed. How is it, will you do as Papa says? Side by side with Papa, you are going to swim to that vessel standing out there at sea. But if you come too near, our feet may clash, so always keep about one *ken* away, and on the way, though you may be stung by the jellyfish, don't be scared or kick about or return to the shore. As to the style, you may use whatever you like, only, when Papa says stop, no matter when, turn on your back and rest your arms and legs. Can you do this?' I said that I would do as he ordered. Then father took the finger-tips and toes of the feet and rubbed them and putting me in the water soaked my head, then said, 'Now we are ready!'

On the way, just as I feared, I was stung by the jellyfish, but stood it. 'Are you tired? Have you a belly-ache?' father called out several times. My reply each time was, 'No.' Then father's spirited order came several times to rest. The colour of the water changed, and it got cold. Father and son began to go farther and farther out to sea. I wished and wished that Otokichi was near me. The waves,

A VIEW OF YAIDZU BAY

YAIDZU FISHERMEN LANDING
A NUMBER OF KATSUO FISHES

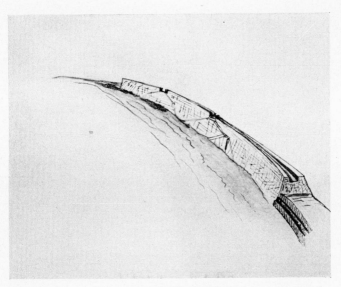

THE BREAKWATER OF YAIDZU

PEN-SKETCHES BY LAFCADIO HEARN

beating against the shore, gathered and broke up into separate waves. I looked at these and at the noisy girls and boys with their bronze statue-like figures, taking tubs and boards and raising piercing voices in their enjoyment. But they gradually vanished and children's voices could not be heard any longer. Even the motion of the water could not be discerned, for it looked like glass. Out into the sea father and son progressed, neither hurrying nor going slow. On turning and looking at the breakwater, it seemed small and low, like a light-coloured sash. Jōnokoshi beach seemed much narrower than I thought. Contrary to this, the ship that looked like a toy from the shore began to get larger and larger and we could see the men on board.

After repeated rests and progressing, we finally came near enough to see the crew laughing and showing their teeth at us; they said something to us from the ship. When quite near, I noticed that this was not a Yaidzu boat. It looked in some respects very much like the Yaidzu *katsuo* boat, but it was different in some parts and much bigger. It was quite strange to see the shadow of the boat on this sea under the hot bright summer sunshine. The colour of the water in the shadow of the boat was very deep blue — sapphire. As we approached nearer, it began to smell fishy. Bronzed faces looked down upon us from the boat. 'It's wonderful you got here!' 'Sa, come up and rest!' 'You are from where?' 'For Tōkyo visitors, you are great swimmers, etc.' 'How old is the child?' We were covered with such queries. 'Eye look to be bad, but he's a brave daddy; fishermen's children couldn't come so far.' All these remarks were uttered in rough language, but they were very sympathetic toward us. 'We'll pull you up, so line up'; but father declined and held on to the anchor rope and rested there and talked to them. The captain, an old man, handed down to us, in a big clumsy cup, some hot sugar-water. 'Don't drop it.' So saying, he handed it to us. The boatmen were fishermen from Enshū. 'Today we are cleaning and getting ready the ship's things so that we can sail from here tonight and tomorrow we shall be out at sea. Yaidzu boats come our way too sometimes,' they said. After a little we parted from them, saying, 'Sayonara!' (good-bye) and swam back toward the shore. Returning, different from going, we did not rest much, and put on more speed also, it seemed, though we were carried along by the waves somewhat, and came to the beach. It was about a half *chō* north of our original starting-place, but we landed safely. When I reached shore, I realized for the first time how tired my arms and legs were. Father praised me very much, saying: 'If you can swim that much, you are quite safe. If it is not in a great storm or in frozen weather or bad changeable sea, if about to drown, you can save yourself.' Afterward, he repeatedly said, 'Don't ever forget the hard struggle of today!'

This took place in the summer of 1901. We took Aki to Yaidzu with us that year. One evening from the back window, we noticed a big spider as large as a walnut making a web about one *ken* wide. Father cautioned us all not to destroy it. In the day we were unable to find what it did with itself, but in the evening it came and settled itself in the middle of the web, waiting for some prey to light on it. Attracted by the light of the lamp, moths, beetles, etc., came and were caught in the web and were wound up by the spider. Some very strong prey would cut loose from the web and try to escape, but the spider would jump bravely onto its back and from the back of the net, with its many legs, grasp and bite it fiercely. We saw this done frequently. One day Aki caught a crab that came crawling up on the board roof and teasingly said to father, 'Sensei, shall I put this on the net? Which is stronger?' He was prepared to be opposed by father, but instead, father said: 'All right, put it on. But it is out of the question, I think, as the crab has a hard shell — armour, like the warrior's. The spider is one that works hard like a farmer. That crab is larger than the spider, too.' Aki, when trying to put the crab on the web, found that the crab's shell, unlike the beetle's, had too much water and weighed more, so it would not hang well. It seemed to hang and then it would drop. The spider got impatient and timid, it seemed. Finally, when two or three of the crab's hind legs were wound up in the web, the spider spun round and round it, making the web hold the legs so that it could not drop. 'This is quite safe,' he seemed to say, and wound sufficient to keep it safe. Even so the strong crab, using its strong pincers, kicked about and injured the web. The spider seemed to think that he could not tarry, and jumped at the crab's head. While the two monsters struggled, something like a broken toothpick dropped on the board roof, which was orange-coloured by the evening glow. Father, who had the glass over his eye, looked and said, 'Ah, the spider has had his leg cut off.' Sure enough the next moment, thinking what it would do, the spider jumped back, crawled up by its thread to somewhere under the eaves of the roof.

The crab, though it had its freedom impeded, hung head down, swinging its two clippers and began to froth at the mouth, but before a minute was up, the spider came down again from its hiding place, and changed tactics by beginning to spin its web from a distance, round and round the crab, intently. It took a long time. The long summer twilight had passed; the sun had gone down in the west, yet it continued, until we had to put the lamp by the window in order to see, as it wound its web around the crab. It did not try to come in direct contact, but from a distance it wound and

wound firmly. When the work was done, the spider
went back to the middle of the web, as we thought
to rest, but it quietly crawled up the web and hid
itself in the bamboo rain-gutter of the roof. Just
below that, the wound-up crab looked like a small
ball made of white silk cotton. In the evening
twilight it hung alone. The spider, while it was
winding the crab, had no mind on the insects that
were drawn by the light of the lamp. Brown moth,
shining golden green beetle — of these, some were
caught in the web. The spider did not mind them
at all, his thoughts seemed to be centred on how
to subdue the enemy that was hanging. That night
father told us about the battle of Amakusa. This
is a great battle between the Bushi (or Samurai)
and peasants — but behind them, the Christians,
and how the Toyotomi-ronin had some scheme
going on which resulted in the battle.

The next day the black spot could hardly be
seen — it was just like a cocoon — the wound-up
crab was covered all over and hung. The spider
came out in the evening and waited in the centre of
the web, but would not go anywhere near the crab
which was wound up and may have been dead. In
the centre of the web rested the spider coiled up,
but he had lost one and a half of his hind legs. For
trial, Aki again brought another crab and put it
on the web again. As the web shook, the spider
thought it was a big prey and rushed up to it,
but it seemed to recognize that it was the same

sort, so it seemed surprised and ran up the web
and hid itself in the bamboo rain-gutter again.
Father, seeing this, said, 'It had a bad experience
in the battle the other day,' and laughed heartily.
Father said, 'Take that crab down and let it go!'
So the tormented crab which was wound up was
taken down, too, and the threads unwound. The
crab was found to be dead, but there seemed to
be no injury anywhere. In the evening of the next
day, father called 'Kazuo, come quickly!' I went
up quickly to the window and saw that the spider
seemed angry and was destroying its web. 'What
is it going to do?' I wondered if it were going to
make a new web. We all watched. Leaving only a
thread hanging from its body, it destroyed all the
web. Hanging only by its single thread, it again
hid itself in the bamboo gutter. Finally, we all
began to wonder, and looking around doubtfully,
noticed, from five to six *ken* distant, there was a
lacework web between the next-door roof and the
persimmon tree, black against a half-moon in the
faint blue sky. Father seeing this, said: 'Patience
has its limits. When at first it thought this place
was all right, it stayed here, but it found it could
not do its serious work without someone disturbing
it. He is a fool who stays a long time in a place
without any hope and being constantly opposed,
to be finally destroyed. That spider was smart,
and taught us the meaning. O Spider, excuse me
for having disturbed your work and given you such

anxiety, but as result, you became more careful —
now you are safe. We shan't trouble you again.
You taught my son a good lesson. Thank you.
After this, be careful only of birds and bats,' he
said.

Father, Aki, and I, on our return from Wada,
while passing through the reed swamp, heard the
cry of a kitten. At first we did not pay much attention to it, but as we passed the tombstones and
were going along the dyke to the left toward Inari
Shrine which stands between the old pine trees,
the cry became more and more distinct, and it
seemed to be coming after us, for it sounded nearer
and nearer. Father was the first to feel strangely,
and we all halted and looked about, but from this
place, which commanded a fine view, there was no
cat to be seen. However, from behind us came a
man dressed in striped summer dress, which was
tucked up behind him, his feet in straw sandals,
with a pole *tenbinbō* for carrying goods on the
shoulder, on one end of which was a mushroom hat
and a bundle wrapped in oil paper, carried like a
gun over one shoulder. In the left hand was a
bundle wrapped with a very dirty *furoshiki* (wrapping cloth), the original figure of which had long
faded. This hatless fellow was hurrying toward us.
In this lonely place, not much frequented by people,
to meet such a person was not very strange. He
seemed like half peasant and half fisherman, judg-

ing from our first glance, but there was nothing like a cat to be seen anywhere. Perhaps it may be up one of the pine trees and crying there, but careful examination gave no result. By this time the fellow had come up to us and in passing uttered a friendly greeting, 'Isn't it hot!' Suddenly, Aki, pointing to the fellow's dirty *furoshiki* bundle, said, 'It's there!' For at intervals a cry of 'Mew, mew!' came from that direction. Our suspicion became a positive thing, for the *furoshiki* bundle began to wriggle and stretch. 'What is he going to do with that cat?' asked father of Aki. When Aki inquired of the fellow, he said, 'These two or three days I have been at repairing ships and the captain wanted a black cat, so I took one, but they did not want a female. I am taking her back now, though I thought of throwing her under that bridge; but that would be a pity, don't you think so?' 'Is she a kitten yet?' 'No, not quite a kitten, but she's young. She has not had any kittens yet,' he said. 'Just let us see her,' father said. The fellow untied the *furoshiki* and spoke to the cat, saying, 'Don't struggle so, we'll let you out.' He took out a black, thin, big-eyed, young female cat. Father said, 'Let's ask him to give us this cat. What do you say?' I bent my head as if in doubt. She was not a very good-looking or a nice cat, and she was so thin and the place where we are to take her was the fishmonger Yamaguchi Otokichi's house, wasn't it? Such were my thoughts. Seeing my cautious looks, father said, 'Don't you like the cat?' 'It's a pity, but she's so dirty.' When I said that, father said, 'It's a pity, so I will take her and pet her up and she will soon become a fine big cat, I think.' Then Aki said, 'She may take Otokichi's fish in the shop.' Then father said, 'So, I thought of that, but she's young yet, so she can be trained.' This cat the fellow was glad to give us. Father, through Aki, gave the fellow a piece of silver, as tobacco money. He tried to refuse, but we made him take it. Though it was hot, the little creature was trembling, and father said, 'You needn't be afraid any more.' So saying, he put her in his bosom and returned to the boarding-house.

Father said to Otokichi: 'This cat, I couldn't stand seeing her thrown away and brought her with me. She may be troublesome, but though I will watch her as carefully as possible, try not to let her steal your fish in the shop. Please let me keep her while I am staying here.' 'Hé-hé-i, please keep her. The black cat is good luck,' he said, and hearing this cheerful remark, father felt easy. The cat was washed carefully and wiped dry. For some time she was wrapped in a comforter and slept. After that, father gave her something to eat. Her two eyes were very bright like balls of fire in the night. Her back, when rubbed in the dark, would show sparks and snap. Father named her 'Hinoko,' spark or child of fire. This thin Hinoko in a week was fatter, and her fur took on more gloss and she

became active and at the same time very mischievous. The evening we brought back Hinoko,
we were afraid that she would go downstairs to
steal fish, so father shut the doors between our
rooms, cutting her off from the outside, and put
her in our mosquito net. But the next morning,
when father got up, he discovered something awful.
Though a box of sand was put in the room, she used
father's precious hat which was on the *tokonama*,
and relieved herself. Father scolded Hinoko, and
the next night he left a door open upstairs, just
enough for Hinoko to go out on the roof, if she
wished. Hinoko soon made friends with another
cat. This friend belonged two or three doors beyond the rice shop, and was a male cat. The two
like good friends played from roof to roof. Hinoko
obeyed father's scolding, so not once did she go
down to steal and eat the fish in the shop.

One day father took Aki and me for a walk.
Passing over the stone bridge which spanned a
stream at the back, and going by a bamboo grove
belonging to a pawnshop, one of the largest land-
owners of the place, we heard 'mew, mew' — a cry
of a young kitten. So father stood still and listened.
'Again a poor kitten has been thrown away,' he
said, and, looking about, we could tell that the
kitten was trying to get out of the bamboo grove,
though its body was not visible, for it was scratch-
ing and crying. Before we could get to the bamboo
grove, we noticed a man leaning against the fence

and talking to a young woman. He was saying something to her. Unlike any of the men of this village, this man had his hair parted in the middle. As it was near evening, we could not see very well, but he seemed to be pimply-faced. The girl had her hair dressed in the Japanese maiden fashion, and wore an apron. Both of them had on summer dress. When we stopped to listen to the kitten's mewing, they stopped talking and helped us get the kitten out of the bamboo grove to the road. These two, breaking and cracking the bamboo fence, and dividing the bamboo and holding it in that position, pulled out the kitten finally. 'I wonder if it doesn't belong to this house,' said Aki. 'It was thrown away; this house does not keep cats,' the cheap hairoil-smelling girl replied. At last she confessed that she was a maid of this house and assured us that the kitten did not belong there, but the place being very convenient, people frequently came and threw their pups or kittens into the grove, much to their regret, at the same time pointing to the fellow at the side, she said, 'Please don't tell anyone that you saw me talking here to this man.' As they had helped us to get the kitten out, father told Aki to give them some money. This kitten was younger than Hinoko, small and black and white. Its fur was the kind that people like. Carrying it back to the house, we gave it food. We took it up to Hinoko, but Hinoko bristled up her hair. I wanted to strike Hinoko.

'You ungrateful thing! You were picked up and this little kitten was also picked up just now. You should love her as your little sister. I thought you would play nicely together with her. Instead you cry, "Wōō-wōō!" and bristle up the hair of your back, and scare the little innocent thing that came later. What do you mean!' I thought thus inwardly and was disappointed with her. But father did not try to scold Hinoko. 'This is natural,' he said.

That evening, when the two were kept together, the miserable little thing was teased by the mean one that came first, so we had to keep them apart. The next morning, when the little kitten was taken to Hinoko, though last night she had acted as if she would like to jump on it, and was put close to her, she simply cried and kept at a distance, and finally jumped out of the window and, going from roof to roof, went to play with the rice-shop cat. Father said, 'It's all right now; she won't tease this little thing any more'; so feeling easy, he took us all and went to the sea. After about an hour we all came back from the sea. I could not get all the water out of my ear, so standing on one leg and hopping about, I went to the entrance. But there Otokichi's wife was holding the little kitten in her arms. When we had left our rooms the little kitten was tied to a pillar upstairs with a long string. 'Why, has something happened?' I asked. 'That black one came back awhile ago and was teasing this poor thing,' she said. At the same time she was spitting saliva on her finger and rubbing the tip of its ears where it had been injured. I felt anger rising in my bosom. Heaven and earth seemed to get hot, my eyes began to blur. I no sooner heard this report than I kicked off my sandals, ran upstairs to crush Hinoko, to step on her, to swing her around and bang her down. As I ran, I heard father calling after me. But fortunately or unfortunately, Hinoko was not to be seen anywhere. Father rushed up after me and said, 'You must not strike or scold Hinoko. We are hiring fishmonger Otokichi's upstairs. Here I am trying to keep two female cats. It was my mistake. Hinoko alone must be troublesome to Otokichi. And again that little kitten was brought in and kept, to be teased by Hinoko. The poor little thing may be miserable. So even today, if there should be someone willing to adopt it, we must give it away.' Just then dinner trays were brought in. Hinoko, who had been hiding somewhere up to now, came in through the window. I wanted to take her and squeeze the life out of her, but she went like a wind to the other side of the tray and settled on father's lap, and like a spoilt thing, cried, 'Mew, mew.' I thought of that poor little thing and glowered at Hinoko, thinking what a cruel thing she was tormenting the weak. I said, 'If I were papa, I would throw Hinoko away and keep the little kitten.' Papa, hearing this, said quietly: 'No, that won't do. You are wrong. Put yourself in Hinoko's position. Animals, unlike human beings, are honest. If a rival arrives to win its master's love, it would do its best to do away with it. Though Hinoko was here, I thoughtlessly picked up the kitten. It was not fair, and I owe an apology to Hinoko. Kazuo said that he wanted to throw away Hinoko and keep the little kitten, but that is not a fair judgment. It's a cruel idea. The previous comer should be respected as such. After Kazuo came Iwao and Kiyoshi, second and third sons. Even so, I did not cease to love Kazuo. I didn't love the new ones more than you. I don't do that kind of wrong thing. In this world there are men who cast aside their own wives and live with new women for such reasons. They have hearts like the devil's. But these people do not tread the ordinary path of life. They should be despised. If Hinoko had done something bad, I should throw her away, even though she was a previous comer, and in her place keep the little kitten. But Hinoko has done nothing bad. Hinoko only teased the little kitten, but that was through my oversight. I unconsciously placed her in a position to tease the kitten. I apologize to Hinoko and will give the kitten to someone. Hinoko I will pet more than before.' At the time I could not grasp father's full meaning and could not understand his feeling for wanting to apologize to Hinoko, saying, '*Gomen, gomen*' (pardon, pardon).

One day a man came from the direction of Tōmé, selling eels, and he decided to adopt the kitten. I felt bad to part with it and wept.

Up to now there had been only one toy shop in this town. A wooden boat was bought for me, with which I played. It was a roughly made imitation of a Yaidzu boat and the price was only seven sen. Otokichi fitted it up for me with sails, mast, oars and paddles, rudder, boards, etc. When it was all ready for sailing, I named it 'Hinoko-maru,' which was written on the flag. But after the unpleasant experience, I tore up the flag and threw it away, and in its place put another with the name 'Yaidzu-maru.' Father, that evening, in order to make a better understanding between Hinoko and me, made me hold her, and, going out and sitting down on the cooling bench out in front of the shop, told us stories of the West Indies, where he kept more than thirty cats, and they kept away the insects and snakes. He, the bad-eyed man, was frequently prevented from harm by them. Then he went on and told various experiences connected with cats.

One day, while father, Otokichi, Aki, and I were walking on the newly made dyke, about two *jō* high, with the cool breeze blowing our sleeves, we wended our way southward. The dyke was made up of great stones and cement, it had a thick stone railing on it, and a stone Buddha about one and a half *shaku* was standing against it. When we looked closely at the Buddha, we found that it had lost its hands and head, and in the place of a head was put a large stone, resting on the shoulder. 'It's a pity! What Buddha is it?' father asked Otokichi. He answered that when the former dyke was here, made of wood and clay, there was a wave-preventing Jizō (or Ksitigarbha, the deity of mercy). So this must be the Jizō. Father, who had heard many fishermen pray, 'Safety at sea,' thought it a pity that here was their god in such miserable shape. 'Let's fix it up,' he said. 'Who owns this stone image?'

After making inquiries, he learned that it was owned by a person living under the back of the dyke, an old woman. To make sure of her permission to repair it, we sent Aki on the errand. She told him the image was said to be that of 'Nami-yoké Jizō' (Breakwater Jizō or Jizō who is a guardian from the wave), but it was not her property. Now it had no owner. At any rate, it was made in the Tempō period (about seventy years past). Neck and hands had been broken long ago, but during the repair of the dyke, it lost its lotus stand, the old woman remembered. She said: 'It was very gratifying to have it repaired. Tomorrow is Jizō-sama's day, so I shall announce this to the old people of the neighbourhood and have them gather here for prayer.' She was weeping with joy.

Father told Otokichi to get the best stonecutter

in Yaidzu and have him look the image over and
see what could be done with it. The stonemason
said: 'It is very difficult to repair it, it would be
better to make a new one, it would pay better.
To make one just that size would take only seven
days, carefully made with stand and all, and the
cost will be ten yen.' Father said, 'Then make a
picture, a plan, of it and show it to me.' Among
my playmates was a fisherman's son named Zensaku-chan, whose face, father thought, would just
be suited for the Jizō model. Father said, 'Take a
look at him well.' The stonemason took a good
look at Zensaku-chan's face, and smilingly went
home. Father, when he was writing home to
mother, made mention of what he was intending
to do, thinking that without doubt mother would
consent. The next day the stonemason brought
the plan, but it was unartistic and very unskilfully
drawn up. It was so unlike Jizō that it could not
be taken for such and did not resemble Zensaku-
chan at all. Looking at it, father wondered and
was surprised. He could not consider making such
a Jizō. A man who drew such a plan could not
make an artistic, sacred-feeling Jizō. The stonemason said that at a certain temple there was one
Jizō that he had made and would show father.
Hearing this, father felt easier, and the mason left.

Soon the old woman came to ask 'When will it
be repaired? It's customary to offer *mochi* [rice-
cake], so please contribute that too; and many will

gather there, so not only tea and cakes, but *sake* [wine], will also be necessary, I think. What will you do in this respect?' As several such selfish queries were made, Otokichi and his wife said angrily, 'Why, what a selfish old woman!' Otokichi continued: 'Sensei-sama [master] is repairing or making the Jizō for the people who work at sea. That much in itself is enough, isn't it? Then to ask him to contribute the offering — you are a little too greedy, don't you think? You have lived in this world for many years, but be careful now not to get divine punishment from what you say. I will contribute the offerings, if you want them, but I will not let Sensei-sama contribute them.' In such manner she was scolded by Otokichi, so she rushed home in a hurry.

When father was considering repairing this miserably broken stone Jizō, many unpleasant things came up to disturb his thoughts. A letter came from mother, which said: 'From the olden days, Jizō was said to be made when a child died, or when all the members of a family were killed as a result of some unfortunate occurrence. So I consider it a very unlucky thing to do. It's not only grandmother and I who think it, but to be assured, I went to the Dōrinji Temple and inquired of the priest, and he replied to that effect also. If you have not been asked, it is better not to do anything with it. Or has Kazuo been carried by the waves and died?' Such a sarcastic letter it was and so full of irony. 'Ho, ho, mamma is opposed to it,' father said. 'As I only wrote Jizō, she has misunderstood me. If I had written more fully, explaining that it was Namiyoké Jizō, it might have been all right. It's too bad.' He wrote at once to mother: 'I apologize from the bottom of my heart. What you say is right; so I will promise to stop. Please feel at ease; pardon, pardon.' On the margin of the letter he drew a picture of a stone Jizō, shedding stone tears. From the mouth of Jizō he put such a monologue: 'I am quieting the waves, preventing floods, that is my duty. I am not the one to protect the spirit of children. But that child's mother misunderstood and prevented my repair. Oh, how sad!' To the Jizōsama caretaker he said, 'I consulted my family about Jizō repair, but all opposed it, so I am sorry, but must decline.' He sent Aki with such a message, and as an offering contributed a little cash.

The stonemason a few days afterward brought from the temple the stone Jizō which he had made, to show father. It really was a fine piece of work. The stonemason said: 'If you make me take the brush, my hands tremble, so that I can't write or draw pictures, as ordinary people do. But with the hammer and chisel, ask me to dig letters or pictures, gods or buddhas, people, birds, images, to chisel them out, I can do them well and show you.' When father heard this, he wondered and thought it strange. He told the mason that he could not have the stone Jizō made after all, and for his troubles handed him some monetary gift.

In his book 'A Japanese Miscellany' father wrote of the 'Drifting' of the hero Amano Jinsuké who lived just opposite Otokichi's house, where each year the swallows came to build their nests. He was the liquor-store master. Father called Jinsuké-san upstairs where we were staying when he heard of the great wreck. He was a grey-haired, well-built, strong old man. In his simple local dialect he related his story. '*Jin-yō-kocchi-ê-koi, kocchi-ê-koi*, [Jin-yō come, come this way!] it seemed to call.' Or, 'It was *Katsuo-no-eboshi*, a kind of jellyfish, the small purple one. When stung by this variety, no matter how thick one's skin may be, he will suffer for three or four days.' He told such stories or repeated the Buddhist hymns: 'Hang down your Mercy's net, O Jizō, between life and death at sea. We are about to sink — save us!' As he recalled, he said, 'Yes, I prayed, and prayed earnestly. Prayed to Ogawa-no-Jizō.' He told his stories in an interesting manner, and to his reminiscences of more than thirty years ago, we all listened with great interest. Father made notes as he listened, jotting down something every once in a while. Jinsuké gave him good material for his writing and it made him happy. Jinsuké was treated and returned home, pigeon-toed, in the fine rain, holding an umbrella over him which had 'Ama Jin' written in thick brush on the paper. He went home to his house opposite, making a great noise with his high wooden clogs. We all watched him as he disappeared in his house. Father said it was a fine story, and hopping and saying something in an undertone, walked around the room, happy as a child.

The next day was clear after the rain. Father took Otokichi as guide and we went about one *ri* to Ogawa-no-Jizō to worship. This shrine was quite large for this part of the country. It was grand. Here the boat boards (from the wreck) were offered. We saw the very board to which Jinsuké clung while drifting. It was placed in a frame and put up in front of the shrine overhead. On it was carved the song of the 'Mercy of Jizō.'

Some time after this, one morning, at the back of our house, we heard a loud noise as of water. Father asked the people of the house what it was and they said it came from Jinsuké-san's go-down, and they were mixing *saké*. Behind Otokichi's house, as mentioned before, were two go-downs painted white, standing side by side. One of them Otokichi rented and used for storing things such as *katsuo-bushi* (dried bonito), etc., and the other Jinsuké rented and used for keeping *saké*. Father was curious to know what was meant by mixing *saké* so he went to the back. There were many *saké* barrels standing in rows, and big tubs. Here, under Jinsuké's instructions, his son and employees of the shop mixed *saké*, alcohol, and water in certain proportions and stirred with boards which made the *zawa-zawa*-like noise. When father saw this done, he gave one big sigh and returned to the house. As he entered his room he remarked: 'Up to this time I had a good feeling toward Amano Jinsuké, who was saved, through the mercies of Ogawa-no-Jizō-sama and Sanuki-no-Kompira-sama, in his narrow escape from death. He has survived to this day, and every day I thought he was doing a good thing and I prayed for continuance of his life each day — but, ah! it was my mistake! I was fooled again — he was not such a good man as I took him for. Ogawa-no-Jizō-sama and Sanuki-no-Kompira-sama, why did they save him at that time? If he had died at that time with the other crews, he would not be doing such a wicked thing as mixing drink with poisonous alcohol and poisoning Yaidzu people.' So saying, he seemed disheartened. After that he would never drink Yaidzu *saké* again at supper. Otokichi's eldest son, Umekichi, carried fish every day to Fujieda and came home toward evening. Father asked him to buy good *saké*, unadulterated, even though high-priced, and bring it back with him. Father had him do this every day while he was at Otokichi's, and told them never to buy Ama Jin's *saké*, as it was poisonous and urged Otokichi to drink the Fujieda *saké* which was bought for father's use.

Father never liked to have our hair cut short.

But while at Yaidzu, our chief object was to go
into the sea, so he permitted it to be cut short.
Father even had his own cut short. The first
time we had it done, we went to the station at
Yaidzu to meet mother, and when she saw us,
she exclaimed, 'Why, it's shameful!' and laughed
out on the platform. Our new student Okumura,
who came after Niimi and Aki, went with us to
Yaidzu in the summer of 1902. He was not like
Niimi, who was awkward, nor like Aki, who was
skilful and tactful. This Okumura was very slow,
but really conscientious. When we were leaving
for Yaidzu, mother gave him instructions, saying:
'At the time of the village festival, Sensei always
wants to contribute generously, but don't let him
spend uselessly. You have charge of the treasury,
Okumura-san, so please be careful. I don't like
to say such a thing, but it's right after our house-
building, so this year is different from other
years, so give less contribution, though it may seem
small, no matter what Sensei says.' Okumura
earnestly promised, and he was sincere in keeping
his pledge. Okumura had a bald spot on the top
of his head, about the size of a two-sen piece. In
order to hide this, he grew his black hair long,
put on cosmetics and pasted it down smooth over
the spot from left to right, thus covering the scar.
But when he came to Yaidzu with father, as we
all had short hair, he decided to clip his short
too.

Father went one day to a poor barber near-by
and let him shave him. The man had hardly
touched his face five or six times when it was
shaved clean, and father was surprised at his skill,
at the sharpness of the razor, and at the good whet-
stone. Father was so attracted by all these, that
he sent his knife to be sharpened by him at once.
It was soon returned, beautifully sharpened.
He tested it on pencils and boards and was again
impressed at its sharpness. The cost of sharpening
was only three sen. 'Only three sen! that is too
cheap. Give him fifty sen,' father told Okumura.
Okumura was always obedient in his response, but
having received instructions from mother to be
economical, though he was not the real treasurer,
without making any remarks he went down and
consulted Otokichi. Otokichi said: 'Things have
their fixed prices. Even ten sen is too much, but
if Sensei-sama said that, then give him twenty
sen.' Then Okumura said, 'That is just my idea
too.' So twenty sen was given to the barber, who
said that even twenty sen was too much, and it
would be God's punishment to take it. But
Okumura forced it on him and the barber returned
happy. Okumura told father of this in a boastful
manner; he evidently thought that he had done a
fine thing. Father said: 'It's excellent art! Such
skill cannot be easily attained, so due respect and
value should be given to it. I don't pay for out-
ward appearance or nominal value of things!

The balance of thirty sen must be sent to the barber for his excellent art.' In those days, with fifty sen one could buy two big *katsuo* (bonito), so fifty sen was worth something. After father returned to Tōkyo, he received a letter of thanks from the barber which father said he was grateful for more than if he had received an acknowledgment from the Prime Minister.

At Yaidzu, father always got up at five o'clock every morning, and called out, 'Chicks! Chicks! Wake up, Chicks!' in a cheerful voice. Putting on our clothes, we rushed off to the sea. After swimming about an hour, we returned and brushed our teeth, washed our faces, and then sat down to breakfast consisting of *miso* soup, raw eggs, cooked beans, pickles — any kind of Japanese food we ate. Half an hour after the meal, my English lesson began; I was made to read out loud and translate into Japanese. After that we went for a swim or walk. After lunch we rested a little, and then went to the sea again, returning after three o'clock, when I was given my writing or dictation lessons.

In the summer of 1904, the time we spent at Yaidzu was comparatively short. This was due perhaps to children's school vacation being shorter, but not entirely. Father was not as free as he was before. He had stopped teaching at the Imperial University and was now a professor of Waseda

University. The Russo-Japanese War had just
broken out, and he was busy sending to the foreign
newspapers and magazines contributions in favour
of Japan. While at Yaidzu, he watched the papers
very closely and was always on the lookout for
the 'extras,' thus keeping in touch with the
progress of the war. When the Vladivostok fleet
came near Japan Sea and attacked passenger and
cargo ships, shooting and sinking them, he was
disgusted. On an evening, father would sit in his
summer *yukata* on the cooling bench in front of
the shop fanning away the mosquitoes, when the
neighbours, fishermen, fish-peddlers, cake-shop
people, rice-shop people, masters and sons, all
gathered around him, asking, 'Sensei-san, do you
think the Vladivostok fleet will be captured?
Wonder if they will escape after doing the mischief? Wonder when Port Arthur will be taken?
Wonder if England will send guns and battleships
to help us?' etc. To all these questions father replied in his pleasant manner, quoting comments
from foreign papers and giving his view of the
present situation in his poor Japanese. One evening father was talking to them as follows: 'In the
future, if Japan should carry on war with England,
Russia will be on the side of Japan, I believe.'

Father liked Tolstoi and Turgenieff. But the
people who attacked the innocent passenger and
cargo ships — these Vladivostok Russians — he
called ogres or devils and hated them. On August

14, 1904, in the evening, as I recall, there was no
wind and all nature seemed quiet, when suddenly
the streets became noisy — and the 'extra'
sellers came running through carrying banners or
white floats with red letters on them, saying,
'Great Victory!' 'Banzai for Japan!' ringing their
bells and shaking the banners, throwing the
'extras' right and left into every house. 'Vladivostok fleet completely destroyed' was the joyful
report. Father said, 'Isn't this a grateful report of
killing off the devils!' and he shouted and ordered
all the lemonade bottles in Otokichi's shop to be
opened and treated all the people who were there;
not only myself and the Otokichi family, but all
the neighbours who had gathered in front of the
shop. The next day's paper reported the number
of prisoners taken. 'Ah,' father said, sighing, and
at the same time his one good eye became moist.
'Ah, did they save devils. Why did they save
them? Why did they save them? What a great
heart Mr. Kamimura [the commander-in-chief] has
— to save even an enemy! It is a fine thing; but the
crew of the Vladivostok fleet were devils. They
don't know how to be grateful, those devils. Better
not to have saved them. Japanese have hearts too
much like gods'. Hearts like Buddha's. Many
bad foreigners who have come to Japan up to this
time to act as spies or otherwise bad have been
handled very kindly, just as Vice-Admiral Kamimura has done and returned them. These for-

eigners, after returning from Japan, all have forgotten the kindness given them and have turned
enemies and have said bad things of Japan, and
look down on the country.' So saying, he seemed
to have recalled something, as he took out his note-
book and made note of it.

After receiving notice of father's death, Otokichi
rushed to our house from Yaidzu just as he was,
without changing his clothes. He was busy helping at Kobudera at the funeral, at the crematory
and bone-picking occasion. While muttering
Buddhist prayers and picking up father's bones
(two persons picking up the same bone with un-
mated chopsticks), Otokichi suddenly remarked,
'Here is something like the cover of *sazaé* [top-
shell] round and flat. What is it?' he asked of the
crematory man. 'That is the knee-cap — in
common called *hiza kozō*.' When Otokichi heard
this, 'Hé-hé-i, is that so? Then with this Sensei-
sama moved his leg and swam in our sea until just
a little while ago — eh?' So saying, he wiped his
eyes with his blue towel to brush away the tears.

IV

MY LESSONS

IV

MY LESSONS

At Yaidzu father began to teach me English for the first time. Of course I could say, 'papa, mamma, good-bye, good morning, etc.' — only a few short expressions. One day, in front of our boarding-house, on the bench with some children of the neighbourhood, I was playing *ohajiki* [marbles], when two students, passing by, came up to me smiling. Other children were too absorbed in their play to notice them, but I, who was born timid, felt suspicious of them. I at once threw down my *ohajiki*, slipped down from the bench, and ran. No sooner had I got down and ran than one of them gave chase, saying something proudly in English. *Baka!* [fool] I shouted and ran into the boarding-house. I did not tell of this incident to anyone, but somehow — who told I never learned — it became known to father and mother. At mealtime, my parents both looked at me very seriously, just as they always do when I do something naughty. 'Don't you want to learn English?' mother asked.

The end of that summer, after we returned to Tōkyo, I was taken by mother to father's study. I thought that I was going to be scolded, but instead father taught me how to stand. When I stood with my feet straight, he would turn my toes out, pull my chin up to make me hold my head up high, chest out in order to stand in perfect position. 'In every country, soldiers all stand in that manner. In reading and writing, if the position is bad, we get sick or injure our eyes, so correct position is very important,' he said. Then making me hold a book with pictures showing up A B C's, A — Ass, B — Bear, etc., he taught me the alphabet, opening his mouth in a queer way and twisting his tongue in order to produce the sounds in English. If I could not do it correctly on the spot, I was scolded very severely. During the lesson time, if my position was changed, I was scolded, so I thought it very strict. I am sorry to say, my first impression of English was not favourable. 'English is hard. It's not an interesting study,' I decided. After one hour of this drill father said, 'From tomorrow, you must do better'; so saying, he dismissed me from his study. That evening I was enjoying myself playing in the garden, because I thought that studying was over for the day, when father and mother called 'Kazuo' from father's

study. 'Kazuo, quick!' Hearing this I thought to
myself, lesson again, but I replied 'Yes!' in a
strangely trembling voice. While climbing the
stairs, half weeping, I said to myself, 'Do I have
to study again?' Mother, who was standing at
the entrance of the door, heard my mumbling and
shook my shoulder. 'Do you hate to study already? You can never become a great man at that
rate.' Father merely wanted to show me the
beauty of the evening glow from the window.
When I heard this, I became not only red from the
reflection of the evening glow on my face, but
from shame.

Father was not the kind to overlook natural
beauty. Even with his defective eye many things
that other people overlooked he would take in —
which everyone thought was very strange. Sun,
moon, stars, birds, animals, fish, insects, grass,
trees, stones, earth — to all these he gave astonish-
ing attention and much interest, and he specially
liked to look in the direction where Paradise is
supposed to be and admire the beauty of the setting
sun. He would sometimes rush out into the garden
and call the whole family to come and watch it.
I, who was absorbed in play, would be suddenly
called away loudly to come and view the evening
glow or watch the procession of ants, or watch the
toad swallow mosquitoes. I considered it a nuisance. And what a sin on my part, for at such
times father would show and explain these phe-

nomena, and end by apologizing, saying, 'Sorry to disturb your play, pardon, pardon,' and planting a kiss on my cheek, would let me go free. Whenever I saw something that I thought would interest father, I would call his attention to it at once.

In using illustrated textbooks my attention was drawn too much to the pictures, so father discarded these illustrated books for the time, and drew on old newspapers, with Japanese brush, large letters about two inches high. Then, with words which were not easy for him to explain to me, he would make me understand by pictures of his own drawing. Thus he taught me my letters, spelling, writing, Arabic numerals, simple words; but before giving them to me, he would plan out every day and write with the brush the lesson for next day.

After father's return from school, I was taught by him for about an hour, but when I did not learn easily, father would remark, 'I teach many hundreds of students at the University, but it is harder to teach only one Kazuo.' The old newspaper textbooks which father used in his teaching, in half a year filled a small closet. After beginning my English lessons, father never stopped a single day, except when one of us was ill. But for a slight cold or stomach-ache, we never rested. Even New Year's, Sundays, and holidays, it was just the same. 'Learn quickly, please, time won't wait; papa's life will not wait,' he said frequently.

After a year, father stopped using old newspapers and began again with the illustrated books, such as 'Jack the Giant Killer,' 'Jack and the Beanstalk,' 'Puss in Boots,' 'The Nursery Rhyme Book,' etc.

At the same time father began on my instruction in English, I started in learning Japanese reading and writing under mother, grandfather, and Niimi. After learning the Japanese alphabet I began Japanese children's textbook number one. At first, mornings were devoted to English and the afternoons to Japanese lessons. Later, when I was seven years old, I began to devote an hour and a half in the morning to English reading, and one hour in the afternoon to writing and arithmetic. Japanese study had to be arranged between these hours or in the evenings. Father began his Japanese at the same time. Father's Japanese teacher was also mother. Father progressed faster in the textbooks than I did. One day father asked me which I liked best, English or Japanese, and I answered, English has so many tongue-twisting sounds, hard and shameful, but Japanese is easy and refined. Hearing this, father laughed. 'Surely Japan is most advanced in some respects — in customs and manners — but I regret to say that in this world we cannot pass through on only ease and refinement. For your experience in entering the world, you may not like it, but it is better in every way to learn the practical English. English is used all over the world.'

Father was very careful about one's eyes. Not only his own, but of anyone else's. He avoided having me read books with small letters. If the print of the books which he had on hand was too small for Kazuo's eyes, he would buy the same books printed in larger types by sending to Maruzen or Kelly & Walsh or even send abroad for them, just for my use. Sometimes, too lazy to light a lamp, I would lie flat on the floor and try to read by the last daylight coming in through the *shoji* glass. If father saw me doing this, he would scold very severely. Even in broad daylight, he disliked to see any of us reading lying on the floor. 'Books should be put on the desk when reading them. If one is reading in bed, hold the book up in both hands. Even though the print is clear, don't ever read by twilight. On dark days, regardless of time, light a lamp,' he used to say. He always told the maids to sew where it was light.

When we began my writing lessons, he ordered a table specially made for the purpose. This table came up to my chest when I stood up. The top board was slanting. There was a shelf below so that the copy-book and pen could not slip. At the top was a space about three inches wide, at the right side of which was cut a round hole for the ink bottle. This desk I was to use standing without bending my head or putting my eyes close to the paper.

Father, because he was very near-sighted, tried

to avoid near-sightedness in his children, and made
every effort to prevent it. This desk was used in
succession by my brothers, but it is gone now.
Father, when teaching me, called out in a loud
voice, 'Kazuo-bō!' and every time, no matter
what I was doing, I must drop it at once, answer
'Yes,' and run to father's room. When in his study
the first thing that he said was, 'Hands?' When
I opened both hands almost always, he would say,
'Oh, dirty! Wash your hands quickly!' In his
room was always a basin, soap and towel already
prepared. After washing them, he would inspect
them and then hand me the book, saying, 'From
here.' During the reading, if I made a mistake or
forgot many words, or gave poor translation, he
would get impatient. 'It's a useless child!' he
would shout. About the time he shouted 'Useless
child,' I would have been slapped about two or
three times. The more I was slapped, the more
contrary I would get; that was my nature. Holding my book with hands wet with tears, I would
get it very much soiled. Father, making a noise
with his mouth, would snatch the book from my
hands and say, 'Wash your face and hands!'
Some days I went through this performance at least
three times during one lesson. In cold weather
after washing my hands, I would shake the water
off onto the stove, just to hear the sizzling sound,
and wilfully take as long time as possible. 'You
wasteful child! It is not playtime now! Quick!'
Thus I would be scolded again.

At ordinary times, except when singing or laughing, father had a voice like a woman's. So, when trying to make me pronounce correctly, he would raise his voice very high, so loud as to shock one at times. If I shouted in a voice like his, I may have pleased him, but I was too timid and scared of father's voice; not only scared of the loud voice, but it made me more timid and ashamed, so I answered in a voice hardly audible, which would make father say, 'Are you a mosquito?' When playing with the neighbours' children, I, their leader, could make a great noise like wild monkeys, but at study time, standing there in front of father, I could not look up to him, and when I did answer, it was with a mosquito-like sound, made timid by his sudden exclamations and shrinking at almost every movement of the arm whose blows I feared. Even now, if in company of persons superior to me, I must be very careful, for I am inclined to wrinkle my forehead and look up to them, which I am told is a very bad habit. This I attribute to the timidity caused by being afraid; or it may be better to say that it was inborn.

One day, when father slapped me, his finger accidentally got into my eye. I held my eyes and did not continue to read. He impatiently said, 'Why don't you read?' 'Papa, finger, eye —' I said, weeping. He, who was always careful about others' eyes, on hearing this was greatly frightened.

Even in my childish heart I felt that it would have been better if I had not told him of it, for he felt so bad. He at once took me in his arms. 'Pardon, pardon! You were bad.' So saying he carried me to a light place in the hall and examined my eyes and, seeing them red, bathed them in clear water and put in eye-water, and afterward kissed the lids of my eyes with his hairy lips. For this day the lessons were over.

Even dogs and cats, if they are scolded for things that they should not do, try not to be scolded by avoiding the hits as much as possible, so as to escape unhurt. Just so I gradually became quite cunning. If father would give me a slap, instead of turning my face away, I would turn it toward him. This, though more painful, proved to be easier. Then I could cry out the louder, 'Eye, eye!' in a loud voice. This frightened father very much at first and he would stop his lesson, but later he discovered my trick and became aware of my naughtiness, so even though I shouted 'Eye, eye!' he got so he would not stop the lesson, but instead would give me a hard slap on the cheek, or spank me or pull my ear.

Mother asked father to teach her English, but he would not. At first she stood beside me at my lesson time, trying to pick up some English. But he said to her, 'You have other work,' thus making her leave. 'If you learn English, you will be chattering needless things with foreigners and nothing good would result thereby'; so saying, he would not teach her. Father's ideas were wonderful, I think so even now. He tried so hard by devoting so much of his precious time to start me on my English at the age of five, then, after several years had passed, he started my brother Iwao at the age of eight, just a half-year before his death.

Though I was a cry-baby throughout my lessons, my brother was just the contrary, always laughing. Father was troubled about this. If father pronounced a word in a loud voice, it would strike Iwao as being funny and he would burst out laughing; while I, on the other hand, would take it in a shameful way, brother would imitate and then burst out laughing, again and again. Watching father's face when he was pronouncing, his mouth, eyes, face all looked so funny, he would say. When father said, 'You are a rude boy,' he took to his heels and ran. Sometimes father chased him and one time broke a glass door. After he was caught, he would get a good spanking frequently, but he was of different nature from me, so took things in an easy-go-lucky way. Nothing troubled him, so he had a better memory than I. If he forgot how to pronounce a word, he would look at the trees in the garden or the sky, then suddenly recall it and shout it out in a loud voice. Whether it was correct or incorrect, he would invariably wind up with a laugh. 'He is a queer little child,' father would say to me.

Outside of lesson hours, brother was frequently very rude. He had no manners and was careless. Father would scold him about it. We brothers had to say, after we were dismissed from our lessons, 'Papa, many, many thanks.' I was poorer than he. About fifty per cent of my study time seems to have been spent in weeping. When specially bad, father would scold in such a loud voice that he could be heard all over the house and everyone knew about it. At Yaidzu, particularly, the neighbouring houses were joined together so that they knew of the scoldings, and the children who were waiting to play with me after my lessons would be taking it in also. 'Why were you scolded so?' 'English must be hard!' they would say, and I frequently experienced great shame this way. If I appeared with tear-besmeared face, grandmother always said, '*Yeré yaré* [poor creature], your lesson was bad again?' Then she would advise me to ask Tenjin-sama (deified scholar) to make my memory better and improve more in my studies. Grandmother said these words so frequently from out of her mouth with blackened teeth that I got very tired of hearing them, so I would get angry and say, 'I haven't bad memory, but he scolds when it is not necessary, that is why. That is the reason, so, grandmother, you pray to Tenjin-sama and ask him not to let father scold me so much' — such a saucy reply I would make that she was surprised and would exclaim, 'Mah! You wicked child!' and she would be disappointed.

When father was teaching at the Imperial University, on Thursdays he did not return home until about four o'clock, so my lessons on Thursdays were short. After returning home he would change into his Japanese dress, and, taking two or three whiffs of tobacco from his long Japanese pipe, would call me to take dictation. He would select a few lines, and if I did them well, it was over in thirty or forty minutes. But while he was out, he left work for me to do translating poems or reading matter of my own selection, and instructed me to show them to mother. At such times I always tried to select the shortest and easiest thing. When I showed them to father on his return, he would laugh and say, 'Oh, my cunning boy!'

Father had the habit of walking up and down the hall with a cigar in his mouth. I can't remember ever seeing him seated on the floor or on a chair when smoking a cigar. On the other hand, he smoked his long Japanese pipe sitting on a cushion by the fire-box in a Japanese room; or, if in the garden sitting on the lawn, he would draw out his short Japanese pipe from its sack and, taking a pinch of tobacco from the tobacco pouch, take a whiff or two from that. So the Japanese tobacco seems to have been taken when he was sitting or in quiet mood and the cigar when he was in motion, that was what I used to think in my childish mind. Though father was very fond of his tobacco, he very rarely smoked during my lesson hours. If it was writing or dictation or copy work which did not require his attention, he would sit down by my desk and sometimes take a few whiffs, but at such times he would always apologize, 'Papa is tired, so pardon,' then begin to smoke.

The following incident took place soon after we moved to Ōkubo. Father wished to have two or three illustrations made of something in his English book, so it was decided to have Mr. Kawasaki, a painter of Japanese style pictures, do them for him. Because of my fondness for drawing pictures, it was decided to have the artist come two or three times a week to give me instruction also. Mr. Kawasaki was a tall, thin man, hare-lipped, and being such a small child I was unable to judge whether he was good or bad for teaching a youngster like me. But at any rate, he was earnest in making pictures. Mr. Kawasaki brought a small pretty brocaded box containing highly scented Chinese ink, one big and one small brush, and some Japanese drawing-papers for me. With these materials, my lessons began. I did not use any copy, but had to make the strokes which the teacher did and learn to move my hands. This was done with the big brush, thick strokes, thin strokes, and gradually I had to make circles. Afterward, I did copy work, taking historical characters, from a collection contained in a thick book which Mr. Kawasaki brought. He would have me draw from

them, any one that I liked. First putting a thin
paper over the picture and holding it down firmly
with a heavy paper weight, I would carefully copy
it. I chose Kojima Takanori, wearing a straw
raincoat over his armour, writing poems on the
cherry tree. I liked this very much and so took
pains in copying it.

One day the teacher brought many kinds of
toys, and said that he would give them to me.
Among them was one that I took a great fancy to,
contained in a glass box. It was Momotaro
(peach-boy), made of clay, attired in military uniform, holding a flag with the inscription, 'First in
Japan,' with a sword hanging at his side, riding a
white horse. His followers, the dog, monkey,
pheasant, rabbit, and bear, all wore armour and
carried guns on their shoulders, knapsacks on their
backs, standing erect. This set of toys I kept a long
time. These I thought were my reward for making
Kojima Takanori pictures well, but it was not the
case, I learned afterward. He came to get material
assistance from my father, a big sum, which father
was not able to give in full, but helped him some,
and with this amount he was turned away. My
painting lessons stopped here.

Those asking for help were not only Kawasaki,
but included Katō and others. If father sympathized with them, he always gave them all the
help within his power. Even though they did not

ask for help, if he saw that someone was in need, he would give it. There were not a few persons who received help from him, but the unpleasant 'hold-up-hands' kind or pretending beggars, no matter whether or not they were near relatives, he would refuse them on the spot. He had only one brother on this earth, named James. To him father wrote an affectionate letter from the bottom of his heart, and sent it off. In reply he expected to get a warm, affectionate reply, but was disappointed in having him take advantage of his soft words and, in an unfeeling way, try to take advantage of him. Father was disgusted with him, so left his brother without seeing him.

In 1902, after moving to Ōkubo, my slanting desk was put beside father's strong desk in the southwest corner of the study. This corner had glass doors on both sides, which opened onto the hall and not directly outside, so the doors were protected from the rain. Still, raindrop-like stains were seen on the glass, but these were my tear stains made when I braced up and turned, leaning against the glass in order to escape the blows when father tried to strike me, and the tears flew there. One day I entered that part of the garden where I was forbidden to go during father's study time. I sneaked in without being seen to pick up some camellia seeds. Hiding behind a bush, which was no less than two feet or so from the hall on the

left near father's study, I peeped, supposing that
father must be hard at work, sitting at his desk
writing. But such was not the case. He was standing on the threshold of his study, and seemed to be
looking at something very intently, but not into
the garden. I wondered what he could be doing.
'Papa wiping the glass of the sash-door!' Thinking
it very strange, I watched more closely, and father,
unconscious of my presence in the garden, was
surely wiping the glass in the door. It was not my
imagination; with his near-sighted eye close to the
glass, he was wiping the glass with some brown
cloth, and every once in a while wetted it with his
saliva and wiped with it. The cloth which he held
in his hand was one of his socks. Thinking that it
was better to use wool for the glass than cotton, I
suppose, he was wiping away the stains of my
tears, and touching them as if they were wounds
and talking out to himself, saying, 'Don't think
me cruel,' followed by a sigh. I left quietly without
making any noise with my feet, not stopping to
pick any of the camellia seeds, and, going to the
place where we usually played, I sat down on the
swing. Everything looked dim. The squeaking
noise of the rings which I had often heard before
sounded very mournful today. That evening I
told mother about father wiping the glass.

The next day, at writing time, father made me
take down the following: 'On the glass-shōji of
papa's room there are little marks like the marks

made by the trickling of raindrops. Those are marks made by the tears of papa's dear little boy. It makes papa very sorry to see them; but every little boy must cry when he begins to learn — and the glass can be washed.'

Father's English lessons to me consisted of poems, songs, fairy tales, Aesop's Fables, Grecian gods' stories. Besides these, Baldwin's Readers, eight volumes; Macmillan's New Literary Reader Books, six volumes. These readers were not read straight through; he selected those that he thought would interest me. I may read Book III today, but the next day I may read from Book II, and again from Book IV, etc.

About one week before father's death, at my request, I was permitted to read from his 'Kwaidan.' For some reason or other, every story that I read I could read and translate easily (with the exception of the parts bearing on insects), so I was not scolded. During my reading and translation of this book, father seemed shy and unlike himself, for he was not severe and would frequently ask, 'Do you like the book?' 'It's easy and interesting,' I would reply, and each time he would smile. Father said, 'Don't tell anyone that I am teaching my son from my own book, as I feel ashamed.' One who was ashamed of his own works kept them all hidden in a closet and kept them all out of sight. The same day that father died, I had just finished reading 'The Dream of Akinosuke.'

Father at one time thought of teaching me French. After he started me, it seemed to confuse my English, so he stopped for a while. Two or three years afterward, in the spring that father died, he thought it was time to begin French for the second time. But just the same, it was not successful. I was always scolded. My active brother, Iwao, was sent to a primary school just across the field at seven, but father wished to take me abroad to be educated, and did not let me go to school until I was ten years old. Being a weak child (very weak between eight and nine) for one reason, I was not sent to the primary school, but was taught at home and chiefly by father. One day toward the close of 1903, when the chilly winter wind was blowing, father returned from his walk as if in pain, and went to bed. In March of this year he had stopped teaching at the Imperial University, so he was a man of no position. That summer, mother was expecting childbirth, so we did not go to his favourite Yaidzu; but he said, 'Next year I will take Kazuo and go to the eastern part of America and put him in some school — and after seeing him settled, will return alone.' That was his plan. During his illness he was attended by Dr. Kizawa whom the rickshaw-man ran and brought. The doctor said that it was bronchial trouble and said for him to lie quiet for some time, so it was thought best to postpone the journey indefinitely.

Thus my trip to America was stopped. To leave me at home was a problem, and mother complained that not to give me a Japanese education would not look well, so in April, 1904, I was entered at the next primary school. In the meantime, father's illness took a better turn and he began to teach at Waseda University. Father's illness, though he was supposed to have recovered, left him weaker than before. He turned suddenly grey and the muscles that easily swung the twenty-pound dumb-bell became flabby. 'We will go to Yaidzu this summer to get back my strength,' he said. That summer, we went to Yaidzu later than usual and returned earlier than we ever did. One month after we returned to Tōkyo, father died.

I was put in the fourth year class at the primary school, but was promoted to the fifth at the second term. Though I entered school, father did not neglect my English. It was as usual, but father and I had to get up an hour and a half earlier in order for him to teach me English reading, but after a month father noticed that using my head before going to school made my head tired, so it was not good for me. English reading and writing were changed to afternoons after getting back from school. For a short while during the worst part of father's illness, my lessons ceased, but after a little he had me come to his bedside, where he taught me reading, arithmetic, geography, and French. After he was considering about putting me into a

school built by Ōkubo District and talking about
it to Dr. Kizawa, the doctor said: 'It's so unlike
you, Hearn, to put your boy into such a primary
school when he has been brought up so refined in
manner. I objected to your putting the second son
there, and now you are thinking of putting the
eldest Botchan there. It will ruin his manners and
he will become very bad.' Father said: 'That's so;
I have noticed that Iwao's manners have become
somewhat bad lately, but not bad enough to worry
about. Breathing the good air every day, mingling
with other children, roughing with the district
children wildly, he seems to me more fortunate
than the children in the city primary schools.
Even for Kazuo, it may be better for his future for
him to see and hear bad speeches. I don't think
that child will be influenced by evil now. It may
be interesting to become a friend of the farmer's
or gardener's children.' Father spoke to this effect.
The doctor said, 'Friends' influence is greater than
that of parents; it's even much greater than you
imagine.' 'Then what school would you recom-
mend for Kazuo?' father asked. 'In Kōjimachi
there is a school called Gyōsei Gakko, a French
Christian school. Their uniforms and school build-
ings are beyond reproach. It is the ideal place for
your boys, I think.' Father looked at the doctor
with a flash in his one eye. 'That "Bateren"
school?' he asked. 'If I had to send him to such
a school, I would first cut off Kazuo's head.' This

remark upset the doctor. When father was a small
boy, he was put into a certain Roman Catholic
school in France. Being of different nationality,
crippled, and with a queer name, 'Lafcadio Hearn,'
he was tormented by the other boys. Under their
very severe rigid discipline, of about two years of
cruel treatment by them every day, he took a great
dislike to the Roman Catholics and just to suggest
such a place was like a nightmare to him.

Father was careful about my physical exercise.
When I was about five or six, he had a swing and
gymnastic bars installed in our garden. They
were not fixed up by any skilful carpenter, but by
Nakamura. This swing was taken to Ōkubo with
all the other things. After father's death it was
still good for five or six years, when it decayed.
When it was fine weather, almost every day we
used our gymnastic bars. We were made to do so.
Father was careful not to jump on the bars or do
any hard exercise himself. He only directed our
exercises. When he wanted to show us something
new, he always had Niimi do it for us first. Niimi
was thin and tall, and just suited for doing the
different gymnastic exercises. Niimi was truly a
clever man. Taking hold of the bar, he could
move his body round and round like a windmill;
shaking like a stick; jumping like a shrimp. He
was so light and graceful on this apparatus that
even now in my mind's eye I can see him going

through the exercises. Father sometimes used to put his hands on the bars, but could not do any acrobat-like tricks. But he would hang on for a long time without any effort. With his big abdomen and big buttocks, he weighed more than he looked. In spite of this, he could hang on by his hands while smoking a cigar.

Aside from gymnastic exercises, we were made to climb the swing rope. When father commanded, 'Hand-over-hand,' I had to climb the swing rope; then, when I reached the top, I would rest there for a while and he would say, 'Hand-under-hand,' and I gradually came down the rope. In this exercise, if I twisted my legs around the rope, I was scolded. 'Learn to hang on only by the hands,' he used to say. When my arms got tired, I would slip down the rope, burning my palms; then he would say, 'If you do such a foolish thing, your skin through friction will be taken off the palm of your hands.' Among my brothers I was the only one who was disproportioned, my arms being very long. This may be due to having been made to do these monkey-like things when young.

This was done on the advice of Captain Mitchell McDonald. He said: 'Some day Kazuo must cross the sea, and on the way, if the ship that he is on should be wrecked, if he can climb down a rope, he may be saved. Swimming and rope-climbing were for time of shipwreck. Against seasickness, a swing is the best thing.' Its use should be freely

practised. This was father's order, so every time
we went into the garden we had to swing until
we got quite tired of it. Captain McDonald gave
father much advice about me. One day he looked
at my teeth, and remarked: 'This boy is cute, but
his teeth are dirty. Use a soft brush and make him
brush his teeth every morning.' Father felt quite
ashamed and said, 'He is supposed to clean his
teeth, but I didn't look at them myself.' From the
next morning, he began to pay attention to my
teeth. Captain McDonald sometimes noticed and
pointed out that my ears were dirty, and after that
father inspected them every day. He also noticed
that I wore my cap too much on the back of my
head. Hats should be worn a little over the forehead.

I will relate two or three incidents connected
with Captain McDonald. After several visits to
our house, he came one day to say good-bye. He
brought me two foreign books. One was a book of
English verses and stories about babies and the
other was a French red-leather covered book.
This book was just what father had been wanting
to get for me — 'Les Contes de Perrault,' illustrated
by Gustave Doré. Father had tried to get this
book from Maruzen and Kelly & Walsh, but
could not get it for us. How Captain McDonald
got it and where, father could not tell, but it was
written in the book, 'To your dear son.' Gustave
Doré's mystical pictures, just as father thought,

inspired me. He thanked Captain McDonald from
the bottom of his heart for the present. The other
book which he brought was 'The Little Ones,' an
English book. There were many pictures of babies
in beautiful water colours. The contents were stories
and verses relating to babies. Father, when he saw
the pictures, said: 'My! It's a present, but it shows
the naval officer McDonald's ignorance of children.
One couldn't tell from these pictures whether they
were babies or goblin-apples.' The verses were so
poor he did not have the heart to make me learn
them, he told mother. When Captain McDonald
came the second time to Japan, he brought me a
box of candy from San Francisco, and brother a
sword. I was sick in bed when he called. Each
piece of candy had a special flavour, giving the
scent of a flower, and looked like jewels in the box.
I was delighted and was very careful of them, eating them little by little.

Captain McDonald sent father several boxes of
cigars after he went to Manila. These cigars were
first class, but too strong and were not to father's
taste. He was sorry that he could not smoke them,
at least many of them. One day Captain McDonald came to the house wearing very pointed shoes.
On his return we all saw him off at the entrance.
My attention was drawn to these shoes, 'Ya! look
at those pretty pointed shoes!' Father, saying
'Where?' took out his glass to take a good look at
them. 'Those are not fit for my strong friend

Captain McDonald. They are not for him to wear. They're more suited for a finely dressed dandy. Among my friends, if I knew there was one who wore such shoes, it would make me feel sorry for him. Don't wear such shoes to my house again.' The Captain laughed and said, 'Oh, I am fairly beaten,' and he never wore them again to our house.

At our Ushigomé house, Captain McDonald came with Mr. Amenomori and stayed overnight. The Captain told my saintly father many rough stories from his experience, of eagle hunting or jumping off a high embankment on his bicycle. He told of the traits of carriage horses; about hitting a saloon keeper on the nose and bending it; he told these stories in a very interesting way, so he always made father roar every time he came. But father, without hesitation, would always caution him not to injure his inspiration. Some people may take this as being very rude or selfish, but Captain McDonald understood him well and took it in the right light.

After moving to Ōkubo, one day father seemed to be lonely, and he sent a letter to Captain McDonald. Father said to mother, 'I wonder what reply McDonald will send.' Suddenly, the Captain, without sending any reply, came himself personally, and as he entered the door, said, 'I received your letter, so I brought myself in reply.' In the meantime, he was trying to bend his big-bellied body to untie his shoestrings, and rushed right up with father to his study, in order to cheer his lonely friend.

Father criticized Captain McDonald's character. 'He has a wide circle of acquaintances, and he has an excellent talent for economy, and is so judicial in his judgment as to be never beaten; a very strong-headed bachelor is this McDonald!' But the Captain held always unchanging, everlasting friendship for 'Poor Hearn.' 'Haven't seen him for a long time. How Kazuo has grown!' Sitting in a rocking-chair, he took me up on his lap and said, 'Give me this boy, won't you? Papa won't let him go? All right, then give me half, only a half. Half Hearn and half McDonald's child'; so saying, he let me down from his lap. Though a very busy man, with various business, after this he called every Sunday. Sundays were his easy days and he usually slept until noon, but he made it his business to come to our house by nine o'clock, leaving his attendant behind on purpose and thus experiencing much inconvenience. But his purpose was to come and cheer the lonely heart of his friend Hearn. Before electric cars were installed, he used to come all the way from Yokohama to Ōkubo by steam-train and rickshaw and made a day of it chatting with father and went home in the evening. After father's illness, strong cigars, long walks, and exercises and long talks with friends were forbidden by the doctor. On Sunday mornings when Captain

McDonald came, my studies were shortened and when he heard me, he would say, whether it was good or bad: 'It's good, it's good, you are doing well. Persevere more and more and try to make papa feel satisfied.' During the lesson, if I made some poor mistake and if father's voice began to get impatient, he would say: 'Don't scold so much! He will learn in time. It's good that he knows as much as he does. If an American boy of Kazuo's age knew as much as he did, they would think he was doing fine.' But father would say, 'But if I don't teach him as much as I can, my life will not wait.' 'Never mind, I am standing by watching him. I am stronger and younger. McDonald is at hand. Don't worry!' he would say, and used to pass it off, laughing heartily.

The swing and gymnasium outfits attracted the neighbouring children and they used to come every day to play, calling me out. Afterward, I was forbidden to let any and everyone come, only certain good friends. One day, a number of children were gathered in the garden, and they began to talk of what they were going to be — Nakamura Jiya's son Seichan said, 'I'm going to be a doctor.' Hearing this, the Ichigaya Prison warden's son Issaku said, 'I'm going to be an army general.' The horse-dealer's son, Danbukuro by nickname, said, 'I'm going to be a navy admiral'; the paper-shop Kenchan, 'I'm going to be a big shopkeeper at Shinanomachi.' The horse caretaker's (*betto*) son

Itchan, 'I'm going to be a school teacher.' Crybaby Kakikō was going to be a policeman. Cavalry officer's son Gō-chan was going to be the King of China. Each in turn expressed his aim in life. I said that I was going to be like father's friend Captain McDonald. Mother overheard me and told father about it, and he thought that it was very interesting and informed the Captain of it when he called. Young Kazuo's ideal was that spirited, overflowing-with-kindness, jolly-hearted man. This coming from me interested and impressed him and he thought it was very cute. Years afterward, when introducing me as one of the employees of the firm of which he was the president, he remarked to many of his friends, 'Kazuo, ever since he was small, took me as his ideal — eh?'

The story at this point goes back a little. When going through our gymnasium exercises, we had to put on our sport shirts, made of white calico with short sleeves, trimmed at the neck and around the cuffs with a narrow border of black about one-third inch in width. On the chest were some zigzag-like designs, and pants to match with a black band on the side. My younger brother had an anchor design on his chest. It was very suitable for gymnastics and I liked it very much. Then, if it got dirty, I would brush or rub off the dirt. But father saw me doing this one day and said: 'It doesn't matter about that shirt, whether you get it dirty or not. We can buy any number of them, so you don't need to take such good care of it. But the ones grandma makes for each season, you must be very careful of. In ancient time, there was one, Shōgun So and So, who was seen folding up his *haori* by his followers. When they asked why he did it, he answered, "If it was an ordinary dress, I would let you fold it up for me, but as it was made by my dear old mother ——" '

Our children's clothes for every season were all made and cared for by grandmother. She was a very clever old lady. Aside from the sewing, she took charge of the cooking and prepared all our meals. In cold weather, grandmother would sit in the sunshine and sew. The skin of her neck, which was white in summer, would be dark in winter from being sunburned. One day, while she was sitting in the hall in the sunshine, mother called father's attention to it. Father, seeing this for the first time, was shocked at the sight. 'How thankful we should be to grandma for the children'; then gently putting his lips to her neck he planted a kiss of gratitude. Grandmother said, 'Not at all,' and smilingly returned a bow. Between father and grandmother there was never any bad feelings, but there was always this gratitude which sprung from the heart, and it made a very good impression on all the family.

Father's library contained several volumes of the

Bible and many books bearing on Christianity.
A year before he died, he started me to reading the
Old Testament, reading parts of it every morning.
'It's not necessary to become a Christian, but one
should read the Bible at least once,' he said. I had
always been taught that books were holy things
and should be handled carefully. Father, mother,
grandmother, everyone in the house, students,
maids, all the old folks, even school teachers, all
made that impression on me. But now, to be given
the Bible to read, with its fine leather binding,
gilt-edged on the three sides, with a beautiful
ribbon bookmark in it — seeing these things, my
eyes popped out in wonder. Besides, a book which
is called 'holy,' I thought must be a very precious
book indeed, and handled very carefully. Among
father's many books I thought this must be the
most expensive and precious one. But very often
books came to father from abroad. After unwrapping them and seeing their glittering fine beautiful
binding, mother and I would remark to father,
'Isn't it a beautiful book!' 'It must be a fine
book!' Then, after looking here and there, glancing through it, he would say: 'Just as I thought.
It's nothing but simple, poor poems; it looks better
than it really is. In reality, if the contents were
fine, it would not be necessary to make the outer
appearance so attractive.' Very frequently, when
unwrapping a book of very unattractive appearance, he would remark that such unstriking bind-

ing contained something which appealed to him
all the more. I have noticed this very frequently.
So in the case of the Bible, I was puzzled. This
was a book pertaining to Christianity which father
disliked so much. It also had beautiful binding
which father disliked. So could it be bad? No, no,
it could not be bad or father would not give it for
me to read. And most books are useful. But what
father tried to explain about the 'holy' part of
this book I was opposed to inwardly. Why should
this book only be called holy. Most books that
were given us children to read were holy too, we
were taught. By putting such questions to father,
I might make him think that I did not want to   .
read it. The Bible may be a book to read, but I
had a strange feeling about it, and I was afraid to
speak of it to father for fear of making him angry,
but finally I made up my mind and told him. But
father, instead of getting angry, burst into loud
laughter; the ceiling and the glass doors seemed to
shake as a result. 'When I was small,' father said,
'I put such a question to my religious old grand-
aunt, and was scolded very severely.' But this
time, father was not going to scold at all. He
seemed more pleased to have such a question put
to him. So kissing me, he went on to explain, that
the 'holy' is just like the Japanese saying, 'My
sect is the most holy to me,' and gave various
examples about the 'holy' meaning. The last time
we went to Yaidzu, he took the Bible along with

the story-books, and made me read a few verses from it every morning.

That summer, Niimi was with us, and knowing that father was not a Christian, he asked, 'Sensei is not a Christian, so why do you make him read the Bible?' Father smiled and said: 'It's the most famous religious book, so I thought it was best to have him read it. I am a good friend of Christ's and I am sure Christ would say "Thank you" to me. There are many supposed to be Christians who are only outwardly so, only so in appearance, making a show of the Cross and bragging about their pure heart. Such are malicious Christians, and they are all over the world. One like me, though very critical, viewing from a different angle, would be called a heretic by these hypo-crites — but He would love me more than all these people, I think.' After making such remarks, one day he went on to say, 'Buddha, Confucius, Christ — all were of their time and place, and, though different, were the same in spirit. They were friends.' Some time afterward, I heard one of father's many friends say, 'A man like Hearn was really a true Christian.' This made a great im-pression on me, and I have clear recollection of it. At Yaidzu, I remember one day, sitting in a proper Japanese fashion, Niimi with short cropped hair, father sitting very solemn with his tobacco box before him, talking seriously in mixed Japanese and English, explaining about the Bible in his usual painstaking manner. This picture comes up in my mind very frequently.

Father was too much of an idealist. To me he was in every respect like a teacher of morals and ethics. People who said father was suspicious or distrustful may have got their impression from his idealistic point of view. It was no wonder, for he always wanted to see the beautiful in everything, and was so often disappointed, so often fooled and taken in by wicked people. He never had a recollection of having done anything bad or mean; but he was treated coolly when there was no reason for it; some called him a person without any University education and a mixed blood deformity; and looked down upon him. On his part, he tried to overlook their abuse. He may have had feelings of repulsion toward them, but he controlled these feelings. For being born with a gentleman's ideals, he was very correct and good-mannered. He was not the kind to be false or to put on style. His was not a manner for society, it was natural to him. He did not try to appear a gentleman by dressing up with silk hat, society gloves and shoes, by using flattering conversation, a smooth tongue. Nor did he have the fine carriage of a gentleman, for he was born somewhat deformed. He tried to make all who came in contact with him feel at home and easy. Even though he met a man in Yaidzu in rags, if the man addressed him, saying, 'It's fine weather today!' or, 'I wonder if the weather is going to turn out well today?' — to these cheerful salutations he always replied in a very polite manner.

Even to birds and animals he was polite and kind. He considered them as friends come from long distances. 'Aren't they happy! By their action and cry they show their feelings, their manners toward each other.' But he disliked people who were rude or did vulgar things on purpose, such as sneezing out loud in public without holding their hands over their mouths. 'What rude fellows they are! How vulgar!' Making such remarks, he would be disgusted with them, and if he saw them, he would be very serious and would not even smile. Then he hated people whose agile, delicate-seeming tongues concealed their sting; or those who coughed very loud or made loud tramping noises with their feet. Though they might be persons of high position and called gentlemen or scholars by society in general, father would consider them as low common creatures.

After reading father's book on 'Travel,' some foreigners, who always find fault with everything, criticized it as being untrue. It was a very cruel criticism to make of one who of all men tried not to live a lie, utter a falsehood, or associate with anyone who was not sincere. I realized, after father's death, that this world in reality was not the world he pictured. In many cases he was too idealistic, so to those who were crooked-minded or suspicious he would appear as a liar. The very trait which father hated, he was accused of having. I should like to emphasize the fact that father, in spite of his having been tossed and rolled on the rough sea of life, was always very polite and treated everybody as lady and gentleman. Sometimes he realized that he made a mistake in doing so, for he only came across a true lady or a gentleman once in a hundred or once in a thousand times. When he did, he was truly glad.

Father was very earnest in whatever he undertook to do. With his lectures at the University; in his writing at home; when walking in the suburbs; at Yaidzu swimming; with my lessons; his love toward mother — in everything he was earnest and sincere. He never complained much to his family, though he experienced more hardship than most people. He had a resigned nature and, though earnest, was very patient too. If after a sincere attempt something did not succeed, he would continue at it for some time and then give it up, saying, 'It can't be helped.' He would not hang on to a thing in a regretful manner, but if he saw some favourable results from his efforts, he would continue until he realized his aim. It was the same with his meals. He was never fussy. He always took what was placed before him in a contented manner. His ideas about books were particular, but about his food, he was not the kind to order several courses. Mother always managed it as she saw fit. Roast beef, roast chicken were among the best things, with milk, bread, coffee, and frequently toast. He sometimes criticized the cooking by saying that it would have been a little better if rarer or a little more seasoning would add to the flavour. These criticisms were said in a very quiet manner, never in an impatient, sarcastic, or unpleasant way.

In the old days in Kōbé, before I had any remembrance, we had a cook named Matsu, but after that time, not mother, but grandmother, always prepared our meals, for which father was always grateful. Grandmother's beefsteak or roast beef became very famous even to one of such gastronomic taste as Captain McDonald. If only bread and butter were placed before him, father would never show an unpleasant face or make any remarks. He would always say that it was sufficient. But sometimes, after he had been writing hard at home, he would absent-mindedly put cube sugar in his soup and pepper in his coffee, or ask what it was that he had just eaten. At such times he was unconscious of what he was putting down his throat.

Father always said that he had the best wife in the world. Not in the sense that she was a pretty, smart, or obedient wife — not in that respect at all, though he had no objections to these qualifications. He was very patient, and no matter under what circumstances, he never forgot that he was deformed, and that made him all the more kind and sympathetic. He always tried to bring out the good qualities in a person, and if he saw some good results he was happy. Such was his nature. Looking at the low bridge of mother's nose and rubbing it gently with the end of his soft finger, 'This is very strange,' he would say, but not in the sense that it was unsightly, cute, or funny. When young, mother was quite plump, and weighed considerable, but father, whenever he addressed her, it was as 'little mamma' or 'small mamma' or 'little wife.' He never said 'big wife' or 'big mamma.' Sometimes he said, 'Mother with smell of lamb,' or, 'My little fat hen.' She is much smaller, weaker, and more tender than some foreign women, he thought. But in calling mother cute or little, it was not to dull his aesthetic mind. Father really considered his wife quite smart, kind, faithful, and tried to guide her in these directions. At times her hysteria was bad and her selfish nature became very noticeable, but these he tried to overlook by considering her finer qualities. If he saw her sewing, he would tell her to lay it aside and read so as to find some material for his writing. So sewing and cooking were left with grandmother. Mother would tell him old stories or read something to him, and he praised her as the best wife in the world.

V

WALKS

V

WALKS

Father was very fond of walking and I frequently accompanied him. I was taken very often to the country, but father's walks were more of an excursion or an outing, for he always went quite a distance. Though very near-sighted, without glasses he would walk rapidly several *ri*, but always avoided busy streets. For one in meditation the country road is better. In my recollection I believe it was about three times that he went into the city. Once when Otokichi of Yaidzu came for the first time to Tōkyō, father, the student, and I took him sight-seeing. Once again, on a summer evening, mother and I and the maid accompanied him to Yotsuya night festival to see the insect sellers. On another occasion, on returning from the Imperial University, we went to Shinbashi Station. At that time there were no street-cars, so mother and I took the steam train from Shinjuku to Shinbashi, went to the restaurant of the station and had lunch, and afterward did some shopping at a near-by bazaar, and by moonlight walked home. When we came as far as Ichigaya-Mitsuke, mother got too tired, so we all returned to Ōkubo on rickshaws from there. These were the only occasions that I can recall. We went frequently in rickshaws to the picture exhibitions held at Ueno Park.

One day, when father returned from a walk, he said, 'Today I had a narrow escape! I was walking along thinking, when from behind a woman screamed, crying out, "Ijin-san, Ijin-san [Mr. Stranger], train is coming!" The warning cry came from a woman with a baby on her back. I was so frightened that I jumped from the rail backward, just as the train went thundering past me. Oh, what a dangerous crossing it was! That woman with her baby on her back! If she had not been there, I should not be seeing your faces now.' Hearing this, mother and the family all shuddered. After that, whenever father went walking, he had the student or children or someone go with him always. Up to this time mother had always tried to persuade him to take someone along, but he said that he preferred to be alone.

On these walks of father's, mother very seldom accompanied him. When she did go, the rickshaw-man always walked along behind. Mother got somewhat stronger after father's death, but while father was living she disliked to go for walks. To father she was always self-sacrificing, but she would decline his requests to have her accompany him to walks in the suburb. The reason was perhaps her stoutness. She was really flat-footed, so was a very poor walker. Our walk from Shinbashi to Ichigaya was probably her first and last long walk. The next day after that she was laid up and had to call in a massager. Grandfather accompanied father two or three times. But he was eccentric and troubled father. 'Say, Sensei, do you like flowers?' He would surprise father in his walks by asking such queer questions suddenly. 'Then I will pick that for you,' and going into a farmer's back yard and saying, 'Please give me one,' without waiting for their consent he would pick a chrysanthemum in bloom and give it to father. If there was a tea-house on the way, he was first to discover it and would quickly say, 'What do you say to our resting here? You must be tired?' So saying, he would rush in and, selecting some cheap cakes here and there, begin eating and rest a long time munching them, so father was much annoyed. Niimi, Aki, and Okumura went with him in turn. Father always tried to take me with him. The brother next to me was taken two or three times the year that father died, as I remember.

One quiet clear autumn day, father said, 'Let's

get out as far as we can into the country today
with rickshaws.' Mother consented to go, taking
me along too. We all went from Ushigomé and
wended our way, without any definite aim, toward
the country. On the way, father examined all the
shrines and things of interest to him. First a shrine,
then a temple or stone Jizō, always getting down
from the rickshaw and studying them carefully.
The country was beautiful, with the golden heads
of rice, over which many *inago* (grasshoppers)
were seen hopping about, and red dragon-flies
were flying right and left. Frightened at clappers,
sparrows would fly upward in thick flocks, making
a great noise with their wings. 'What is that man
doing there?' I asked, pointing to an object, which
turned out to be a scarecrow. 'Ah, another scarecrow!' I would exclaim, pointing to another object,
which, on better inspection, I found held a pipe in
his mouth from which smoke was rising and had a
towel tied around his head. It turned out this time
to be a farmer. 'Ki-ki-ki-i!' Thus shrieking something went flying through the air, and it was the
butcher-bird. Then we saw something bright red;
was it persimmon or snake-gourd?

Completely surrounded by a thick grove of cypress trees, we came to the village shrine. We
heard the cheeping and chirping of some bird,
which father said was the cry of the *hiyodori*
(brown-eared bulbul). We came to a place where
the road was too narrow for our rickshaw to pass.

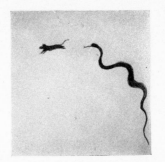

THE WEEPING JIZŌ (STONE
BUDDHA) IN YAIDZU

THE POOR MOUSE

LANDING THE BOAT

PEN-SKETCHES BY LAFCADIO HEARN

Beyond the rice paddies the leaves had turned, showing varying colours of red, brown, yellow, mingling their beautiful tints with, here and there, evergreens and deciduous trees. Seeing this, father exclaimed, 'How beautiful the mixed woods! What is the name of that place?' Our rickshaw-man did not know the name of the place, so he asked of an old woman with a sickle. She said, 'Ōkami-Dani' (Wolf-Dell). I wondered if the wolves dwelt here in the old days. I recalled the story of 'Little Red Riding Hood' which father had had me read recently, and, looking in my direction, father said, 'All the better for eating you with, my dear!' which he kept repeating in a comical deep voice, smiling. Though I was taken there with father and mother, I have not the least idea where Ōkami-Dani is now, and wonder what changes may have taken place there since our visit.

Ochiyai-mura was another place where father liked to go. We wandered in this direction frequently. In those days there were only farmhouses scattered around, with flowing wells where we could get clear nice water to drink. At home, whenever father felt thirsty, he went to the kitchen or well and drank down gulp after gulp of water from a bamboo dipper and enjoyed the drink. But he loved the moss-covered wells, overflowing with clear cold water, so whenever he saw one of them he could not resist the temptation to stop.

In this way he became acquainted with nearly all the old men and women of the farmhouses. At that time nearly all the roofs in the village were thatched. One tall chimney rose up from a crude brick building — it was the crematory. The chimney stood behind the copse woods. Pointing to it, father would say, 'I will soon become a smoke and rise from that chimney.' Every time father made that remark, it used to make me feel sad and resentful, and as I watched him from behind, plodding along with stooped shoulders, his silvery grey hair showing from under his hat, his remarks cast a gloom over me. On returning home from our walk, mother always came to the entrance to greet us, asking, in her customary way, 'Where did you go today?' Father would reply, 'Ochiyai-mura,' and I would add, 'Papa said again that he was going to turn into smoke and come out of that tall chimney today.' Then mother would caution him, saying: 'Papa-san, don't say such a thing to little Kazuo. It's better not to. Nobody feels good in hearing such a thing.' Then father would apologize, saying, 'Pardon, pardon, but it's really so.' Then mother: 'No, it's not true. You must live a long time yet or we would be troubled.' 'But I know my own body well. It will be hard for me to see Kazuo enter the middle school,' father said. 'What a foolish thing! Don't you want to see your grandchildren?' mother would ask, and father reply, 'Yes, I should like to see them, but it's very difficult, mamma.' 'If you say such a thing, it will really become hard. You must make up your mind that you can truly see them,' mother would say. 'Thank you, I will ask God to that effect. Ha, ha, ha!' My parents, carrying on such conversation, used to make me feel quite uneasy and I too offered prayer in my heart, asking God to let father live for a long time.

One refreshing, calm autumn day, after we moved to Ōkubo, father and I went for a walk. He was greatly absorbed in something, so instead of going the usual way into the suburbs, he wended his way toward Shinjuku Oiwake Street. The Shinjuku of those days was a dirty suburban wagon road, covered with rolling dust as the carts and wagons passed. Father said, after a little, 'I made a mistake in the road. Let us run away from this dirty road to the pretty country road'; and he began going quickly in the direction of the country. Just at the end of Shinjuku where Tsunohazu begins, three queer-looking men came and stood in front of us, speaking in loud voices, and sauntering along. They were all scoundrels of the locality and drunkards at that. I could take them in at a glance. None of them wore hats; they wore *awase* (spring or autumn dress), with black neck-cloths, brown sashes tied in front, barefooted, in sandals; towels thrown over their shoulders. Two of them were eating *oden* on sticks, shouting and

tottering along, an incorrigible, oppressive-looking
group. 'Bad gang,' I thought. 'They will surely
say something rude to papa.' And as I had my
suspicions, I cautioned him, saying, 'Papa, bad
men have come. Be careful!' 'All right,' he said,
and we pursued our way. Just as I had thought,
the fellow with the potato *oden*, seeing father,
shouted, 'Ya! Ijin [foreigner] has come.' Then the
one with *konyaku-oden* came staggering up to
father and, peeping into his face, said, '*Bélo-bélo-
bénbéro-bé!*' and shook the *oden* right near father's
high nose. The next minute, before I realized
what was going on, the *konyaku-oden* fellow was
on the road, kicking up. Whether he sat down by
himself or was knocked down by father, I should
like to know even at this date. Father then said,
'Come on, darling,' and we walked on. One of
the rascals shouted, 'Brute! Ya, you wait. You
ruined my one-and-a-half sen oden!' These vaga-
bonds came chasing after us, uttering foul remarks.
Father stopped suddenly and looked back, both
fists clenched, standing at guard, and stared at the
three. I looked up at father's face and felt a cold
chill run up my back, as I wondered if this really
was my father. His expression was such as I had
never seen up to this time. The year that father
died, when he had his picture taken, he had the
same frightful expression, and, looking at it closely,
I felt that he should not have had his picture taken
with such a cross look. Again, when I had done

something naughty and he was about to scold me, his face was fierce like that, but this time, of all his fierce faces that I have seen, the one he gave those scoundrels was the worst. I was stunned for a moment by his looks. 'What will happen?' I was very anxious, but at the bottom of my thumping heart, I felt that all would be safe. They will all be thrashed pretty soon by father, I firmly believed. His eye was bad, but he was as quick as a squirrel. He would sometimes wrestle with young and active Niimi or Yaidzu fishermen, and make them groan and perspire as a result of their struggle, but he would be calm, without changing colour, and call out, 'Ho, ho, a little more?' And his arm seemed to be rooted to the matting and could not be moved. He was much stronger than he appeared to be. I knew this well, and watched. 'What rude fellows!' So saying he turned and resumed his walk. But from behind one of them remarked, 'What a fierce face he made!' 'Why, he has only one eye. Say, it's foolish to jolly a foreigner. Come on, come on.' Father's face was more narrow than round, with small mouth and pointed chin, a feminine, gentle face — but this time all the gentleness disappeared. I feel strange, even to this day, thinking of father's fierce face on that occasion. His fierce appearance, I believe, was due to his bad eye. When it was widely opened, it seemed half of his face became an eye. It was a very strange, popping eye — and was black and the bad eye would shine like a silvery fish-eye. It made a bad impression on one. I used to see the one-eyed Ichikawa Danzō, the famous actor, and felt this very deeply. Over father's eyes were easily moving, black eyebrows; between the two eyes, a high-bridged eagle-like nose; under the nose was a grey moustache. When angry, his lips quivered; from between the lips could be seen tobacco-stained, uneven teeth. These, together with his big defective eye, helped to make his appearance fierce.

Father used to request me to tell him if I saw anything interesting or rare, and while walking, I would often call him and show something to him — grass, insect, shrine, temple, Jizō or some other stone Buddhas, votive pictures, etc. One day, while the building of our house was going on, the head carpenter asked us to send some afternoon tea materials with him, so Aki was sent with him from Ushigomé to Ōkubo and I went along. On the way we noticed, on one of the telegraph poles on the street, a picture of a nude woman that someone who had too much time hanging on his hands had drawn. It was the kind that one sees in old coloured prints — a woman with Japanese coiffure, and lines radiated from various parts of the body, giving some sort of explanation of the parts — especially of the breasts and abdomen and hips — at the end of the lines in small characters. Aki stood in front of it reading every detail of it, and once in a while he burst out laughing and seemed to find it very funny. When I inquired what it was, and asked him to read it, he only said, 'It's something children can't understand,' and would not explain. 'But it seems to be funny as you are reading it alone.' When I said that he replied, 'No, it's nonsense — *sa*, let's go,' and he went on. After two or three days, Niimi and I went on an errand to the Ōkubo building place, and that grave, sedate fellow, just as Aki had done, stopped at the telegraph-pole picture and read all the explanations and he, too, laughed, but he would not tell me why he laughed. At any rate, I thought it must be something very interesting, so I determined to call father's attention to it. I must surely show this to papa, I decided. At supper-time that evening, I told him, 'Near Ōkubo Marquis Maeda Compound, there is a picture on a telegraph pole which seems to be interesting, as Niimi and Aki both laughed when they looked at it.' So father said, 'Then if we pass there some time, be sure to call my attention to it.' One day, as father and I were out for a walk, on our return we passed by this pole. I thought, now, I must show that picture and please father. I stopped in front of the picture and called his attention to it; he was walking a little ahead. 'Papa, this is the picture.' Turning back, he put his one eye near the telegraph pole, but jumped back with a start as if

someone had pushed him, at the same time exclaiming, 'Oh, damn! What a foolish picture!
This is a very vulgar picture made by a low mind.
That kind of thing, don't look at. You know the
story of the three monkeys — "See not, hear not,
speak not"?' He took my hand and rushed on.
After I returned home, I went to the students'
room and reported to them the experience; one of
them said, 'Ya, did you show that picture to
Sensei? Wa — that's terrible. It's funny, it's
funny!' The other student then said, 'To show
that to Sensei was bold. Wah — ha, ha, ha!' And
they both rolled on the floor, laughing and striking
their sides. That evening the students were called
up by father and were given precautions on such
things. On their way to their room, while brother
and I were playing, they passed by, casting a
reproachful look at me, and remarked, 'Kazuo-san,
you have no common sense.' Soon after that, I
saw them go out taking a lantern and a knife. It
was at father's orders, to go and scrape that shameful picture off the telegraph pole.

Father did not care for the general cemetery at
Zōshigaya; he liked better the Yamadera (a temple
in a mountain) Cemetery on Mount Kōya, Kii
Province. He often mentioned this. But he had
made up his mind that when he died his body
should be cremated in the crematory at Ochiyai
village, which had disfigured the beautiful village.

After his death he did not imagine that people would try to carry out his supposed wishes by surrounding him with children, grandchildren, relatives, and friends in a big house and make a big show of it. He was not the kind who said that when he died, he would like to have it announced in all the newspapers, not only Japanese but all over the world, and to make the funeral as grand as possible. He was far from that. He had frequently said that he wished his ashes to be put into a jar, with about three sen in the end, and have it deposited on some temple hill — that was the best way. So, though he is resting now in that tasteless Zōshigaya Cemetery, without complaint, he must be saying, 'It can't be helped,' and resting in peace, in contentment.

Whenever we were out walking and we saw a shrine or a temple or Jizō, father always dropped ten or twenty sen, sometimes fifty sen, into the offering-box. Not that he prayed for the prosperity of his family or for eternal peace, or for increase in the royalties from his books — his offering was not done in that spirit. He only wished to make a simple contribution from his heart. 'I saw a very old, interesting little *torii* today at a shrine, and I contributed a little,' he would say. Or, 'I saw a cute stone Buddha, so I contributed a little.' After coming home from his walk, while mother was brushing the dust from his clothes, and hearing the money jingle in his pockets, he would frequently make these confessions.

About two weeks before father's death, he took brother and me for a walk. On our return lights began to appear here and there in the houses. As we hurried along Ōkubo Street, someone called out, 'Where have you been?' On looking back, we noticed that it was Iwao's classmate Kobayashi, of the second year primary school; a son of a gardener, if I remember. 'We went for a walk,' said Iwao. 'Why?' 'Because walking is walking!' 'Funny!' 'It's not funny at all,' said Iwao. Right behind us, Kobayashi was carrying on such discussion. He was in the second year primary school, but dirty-nosed and stupid. Kobayashi could not grasp the meaning of 'walking' in his simple mind. The next day brother said, 'Niisan [elder-brother], today at school Kobayashi asked me who it was that I was walking with yesterday, so I said, "It was my elder brother." "I know him, but who was that with the moustache and in foreign clothes?" he said. I said it was my father. At this, Asakura shouted from near-by, "Oi, Kobayashi, Inagaki's father's moustache is not black, is it? What colour was it?" Then Arai shouted, "Isn't it red?" Kobayashi said, "No, it is white." Then they all shouted together, "Old man's child! Old man's child!" And they all teased me. If Kobayashi had said it was red, then they would have said that I was "Ijin's" child and tease me thus, wouldn't they? It was quite fortunate as it was,' he said, as he related this school occurrence. Hearing this, I thought it would have been better if they had shouted 'Ijin! Ijin!'

Father's moustache was white, just as Koba-yashi had said. He was old-looking for his age. After his illness, his cheeks had sunken in, his hair and moustache turned grey, and he could not swing his heavy dumb-bells as he used to or go for long walks, which Dr. Kizawa told him not to take any more. But this summer, he swam well at Yaidzu, and when I did some mischievous thing or was poor at study, he could still slap me hard. At walking time he was just the same as before, it seemed to me, quick-footed as ever. He did not seem old. 'His hair and moustache may make him look old, but he is not an old man. He isn't going to die yet. Papa won't die until I grow up.' I said these things inwardly in my little heart. As for brother's mischievous classmate — that feeble-minded Kobayashi seeing father's white moustache and calling him an old man — I told brother that 'I would lick those fellows that said papa was old, tomorrow.'

VI

AT ŌKUBO

VI

AT ŌKUBO

Tomihisacho, Ushigomé, was located just behind the old temple, Kobudera, as I have mentioned before. The chief priest having changed, they began to cut down the old trees on the hill to sell for money. Inmates of Ichigaya Prison began to work every day around our house, putting dirt on straw carriers and dumping it into the carts, and making bonfires of old pegs. On his way to the University, or during his walks, father was obliged to pass along the streets where they were laying water mains or sewer pipes. The place was in a constant upheaval. These unpleasant things made him want to remove to some other place and we looked here and there for a house for rent. Mother had always wanted a house of her own, but father did not have any idea of buying a house here and settling down. He always said, 'Let us return to Matsué or Oki-Island and spend our days there or

spend the rest of our lives on Mount Kōya.'
Though Matsué was mother's birthplace, she did
not like it. In the first place, it was too small.
Then it was troublesome, for there were many
people there that she did not like. At such times
father used to say to her, 'When you were young,
you had many troubles there, that is why you feel
so, but Matsué has many good people. Mr.
Nishida, don't you think he is good? Then the
ōhashi [bridge], the sound of clog noises over it;
Lake Shinji with its evening glow; Atagoyama
moon; Tenjin Shrine grounds; Manjuji Temple
Cemetery — all have their attachments — such a
nice place.' He would say these things in praise of
Matsué.

But contrary to father's wishes, mother wanted
a place near Tōkyo which she could call her own.
Mr. F. was experienced in the common affairs of
the world, such as making matches, finding em-
ployments, acting as house or land broker — he
liked such things very much and he called himself a
'knowing person,' and he cleverly passed his days
thus on this earth. Through him mother found a
one-story Japanese house in Ōkubo, a suburb of
Tōkyo.

After buying the place, mother had father's
study, her room, dressing-room, and parlour added
on. Mother went every day to inspect the building
of these additions. She was so active, but it was
only during the building time that she went out,

whether father was at home or not. Father said, 'You may break down trying to do so much. Be careful!' He was anxious about her health. While she was out, the maids' voices even changed their tones; little brother's rompings showed more might and main. They took advantage of mother's absence; it may have been all right for them, but the one who suffered in consequence was father, and then I. At nights, when mother used to stay at home quite settled, after meals we enjoyed ourselves with the two parents, talking happily or singing English and Japanese songs. They used to sing with us and we thus passed many happy hours together. But mother at that time went out frequently to see Mr. F. or the head carpenter or fortune tellers. On such occasions I felt as if I had lost something, and had a reproachful feeling and rather than having to look after the house, though the places where she went were not interesting for me, still I thought it better to go than be left at home.

On this day, the cold north wind was blowing, and mother was going out again in connection with the building, to see the head carpenter and the lumber dealers to select the ceiling boards and *tokonoma* pillar. Again she was going to be out; I felt discontented. During her absence the only person to give me any thought was father in these days — grandmother was thoughtless. Though I had asked mother to take me along, she had refused, saying, 'Today is too windy and so it's not good for you.' Then I begged, 'Please put on all the clothes I have and take me.' 'I can't do such a foolish thing,' she said. This time something within me created a rebellious spirit, and I thought to my-self, 'Of all people staying in this house, I am the one most concerned about mother and I am the quietest,' but even after such pleadings to repulse me as if I were a nuisance was too much for me. So I determined that when things did not come her way, mother always got hysterical. All right, today I will do all I can to be naughty, and made up my mind to get a good scolding. In front of the entrance I cried and stamped about, feeling lonely as if left helpless. A cursed, queer, indescribable feeling came up. Making up my mind to rebel in this matter gave me an agreeable feeling. It was my first experience. 'Little brothers are staying home quietly; you are the eldest, why this action?' mother said. All those who came near me re-proved, but I cried the louder.

While I was making this racket, I began to think that I might fall over, like mother, grinding my teeth, but kept on. Just then someone came and picked me up gently from behind. It was father. He took me to his study. No one came to apologize for me, so I made up my mind that I was in for a good spanking, but strange to say, it was not so. Quite an unexpected thing happened. Instead of scolding me, father covered my cheeks with kisses

and quietly said: 'You must not make such a
noise and prevent mother from going out. Even
though you tried to stop her, she's the kind of
mamma that won't stop. She is working hard to
make papa and Kazuo a new house. You may be
lonely, but draw some pictures and wait quietly for
her. If you are going to draw a picture, I will give
you this.' So saying, he gave me some drawing-
papers. 'If this room is warmer and quieter for
you to draw pictures, you may put your desk by
papa's and stay here,' he said. I stayed in his room
and drew pictures on several papers on both sides
— ships, trains, soldiers, horses, etc. These were
the things I was always proud of drawing, but on
one of them I drew several carpenters at work with
their heads bound with towels, busy with their
saws, planes, chisels, hammers, etc. Father praised
this one, saying that it was interesting.

After making pictures, I left father's room and
came downstairs. Four or five hours passed, and
mother did not return. Outside, the cold wind was
blowing. Brothers went to bed. Grandmother
said, 'Mamma must be cold out in this wind. The
wind does not let down at all. It must be past
ten o'clock; isn't she back yet?' So saying
anxiously, she fell asleep before we knew it in the
kotatsu (a kind of heater). I wondered whether
the rickshaw in which mother was riding had
turned over. The timber merchant's place was said
to be near the river; I wondered if mother was not

blown over into the river with the hood over the
rickshaw, or just as we have seen it done in the
theatres — if bad men had not come out from some
concealed place and cut mother, taken her money,
and run away. The head carpenter and Sōhachi-
jiya may be strong, but if they were attacked by
armed men in great numbers, they will be over-
come. I was thinking in such a way and was
greatly worried. By and by, I heard father coming
down. Seeing me, he said, 'Kazuo, you are not in
bed yet? It is past eleven o'clock! It's bad for
your health, so go to bed at once.' I changed to
my nightgown and went to father and said, 'Papa,
good night. Pleasant dreams.' Father said, 'The
same to you. Good night, darling!' So saying, he
drew my cheek up to him and kissed me. 'Tonight,
I will be on the side of Kazuo. Really, in this cold,
mamma's return is too late. After she gets back, I
will scold her.'

Just then we heard a commotion downstairs,
and it grew nearer. Ton-ton-ton noise was heard
on the stairs and mother appeared, apologizing for
her lateness, in the meantime taking off her shawl
and coming into the room. I said, '*Oké rinasai*
[honourable return], wasn't it cold?' When mother
left I was very naughty and she resented it or
something, at any rate she was not pleasant, and
said, 'Are you still up? Why don't you go to bed!'
She said this in a severe tone, giving me one cold
glance. Father touched mother's nose and cheek

with the back of his hand and said, 'Oh, how cold! It's bad for your health. Is the house so precious? Isn't your health more precious? You are the children's mother; your body is very precious.' So saying he quietly reproved her. 'Kazuo was anxious about you and stayed up until now. Don't blame him for being anxious.' He showed her then the picture which I drew of the carpenters, and for the first time she showed her smiling face to me. 'You were anxious because I was late, were you?' she said in response to father's mild reproval, but she did not mind my reproachful look at all, only went on rattling, '*Jindai-sugi*' (cryptomeria japonica) — she looked over for the wide ceiling boards and *tagayasan* (Indian ironwood) and other materials for the house she had purchased and was delighted at the outcome of the purchase as she had made a good bargain.

Just as I have said above, father bought the land and house at Nishi Ōkubo and had the additions put on, but he was quite indifferent about it. Everything was placed in the hands of mother and the head carpenter. Of course, this location, house and land, was bought in mother's name, and everything was done according to her wishes, so it was quite different from father's taste. Besides, after the great earthquake, father's library was all removed, as I have mentioned before, through the kind suggestion of the late Mr. Nannichi, to Toyoma High School. After that the house underwent changes. To carry out father's wishes at this original Ōkubo house and property was difficult. The house could not be shown to the public as Hearn's dwelling, for he had nothing to do with it. The things which were considered precious were not typical of him. He disliked such display. When the building was going on at Ōkubo, the only thing he said was, 'If you are going to build me a room, make it light and warm.' That was all, and he never gave any other instructions. Finally, after it was made, he said, 'Moving time is good enough for me to go.' So saying he never went near the place, except at the ceremony of roof-raising (*tatemaé*). Mother said, 'If you don't come, it will not look well,' so forced him to go. His Japanese name, Koizumi Yakumo, was written in large characters on the main beam, and with Shintō ceremony, carpenters chanting something lively and clapping their hands, the beam was raised with other decorations on top of the roof. 'Ho, ho,' so saying, father put his glass to his good eye and watched the ceremony. (In years to come, if the roof of this house should be torn down and they should find the name of Koizumi Yakumo written on the main beam, I wish it understood that it was not Yakumo's house, but mother Setsu's in reality.) As the finishings were going on, mother said to father, 'Shall I put fixed shelves in the study wall for your books?' He said, 'It may be convenient, but if I should die, you may have to turn the house

over to some other party, in such a case, if the
shelves are fixed, the person who buys the house
will find it very inconvenient.' Thus saying, he
would not let her build them in.

We moved to Ōkubo in March, 1902. Father
saw his study room fitted with the smelling of new
tatami (mats) and wood. Through the window
from the garden came the sweet odour of plum
blossoms. Shutting himself in his study, he began
to arrange his books. I helped with mother. An
uguisu (nightingale) came near our window and
began singing continuously. Mother said: 'Isn't
it poetical, to have the nightingale come and sing
to us its song of welcome? It seems so happy.'
But father said: 'What a cute bird. When I hear
that little voice in this house, I wonder if I can live
to hear it more than three springs. It's very difficult, I think.' On hearing his remarks, mother
would be disgusted and say, 'My, how foolish!'
It was just two years and a half after we moved to
Ōkubo that father died, September 26, 1904.

After the house was completed, one day, the
American paymaster, Mr. Mitchell McDonald,
came to visit us. 'You have built a fine house,
everything included. How much did it cost?' he
inquired, to which father replied 'I am an adopted
son. Why should I know how much my wife's
house cost?' It was not a reply of sarcasm — he
was not hiding the facts — he never asked mother,
so he did not know.

Father was a very unselfish, frank person; he
never let regret or attachment block his way. At
some universities, teachers were obliged to retire
at a fixed age, but some objected and wanted to
hang on. Father loved the students, but he did
not show any such action of attempting to be re-
instated (though he was not retired on account of
his age). At the death of Mr. Nishida and Dr.
Toyama and others like them, who were men of
sincerity and true friends, father was sad.

It is said that, during the Russo-Japanese War,
in order to draw the sympathies of the world to
Japan, father devoted his time to his pen. At this
time, during this war, the pen had great influence
and could turn the public views one way or the
other, so he gave great aid to Japan in this way.
After his death, in the beginning of Taisho period,
a posthumous honour was conferred on him by the
Emperor.

It was always father's nature to take sides with
the weak, so with small Japan he had great sympathy — his naturalized Japan, his own country.
This was dearer to him than any other country.
Rewards or honours were far from his object.

He opposed these people who go to historical
places or noted public places on excursions and
dirty the place with soot and other ruining things.
'These capitalists haven't the least regret at destroying noted places, historical spots, by cutting
railways through them and destroying nature,' he

would say. He hated those traitors to their country who carried on business by giving great commissions to high officials and bought the Order of Merit through their influence.

Father designed our family crest. He selected the white heron, the bird that looks so pure and undefiled. He himself was a pure, straight-minded man.

Captain Fujisaki was sent to the front soon after his marriage. He was connected with the Manchurian Army Headquarters and was Field Marshal Ōyama's adjutant. When he came to say farewell, he said, 'This may be put in the family Buddhist shrine,' and left his photograph with us. Looking at it, father said: 'What a bright face! No fear, you will surely return with honours. The Russian soldiers are big, strong fellows, so never be off guard.' 'Ha, thank you! The big target is easy to shoot,' he said, laughing. To this remark father listened with hope and cheer. Fujisaki-san's father was an old Captain, G. Fujisaki, who afterward went to the front. At that time Ōkubo was full of soldiers and gardeners. Neighbouring soldiers were being sent off gradually day by day to the war.

When father finally stopped teaching at the Imperial University, mother said, 'Father is leaving the University. Papa will not let us suffer, but as we have just finished building and the

income will be less, you must not be as extravagant
as you have been.' 'Ha! we are going to be poor,
are we?' I inquired. Mother said: 'Somewhat.
Papa says that he can get about the same amount
from his writings as he did at the University, but it
is different from the University pay. We have no
regular income. We must wait some time before
he gets paid.' For one who was poor at calculations
and so young, I could not understand such family
economics. But I could see that mother was down-
hearted. I was not the one to be able to give her
any support or comfort, even with words. Grandmother frequently said, 'Pray for Tenjinsama's
help,' and I began to think seriously. Father was
particularly quiet at this time, but he had many
callers. Most of them were from the University —
professors, and heads of departments, secretaries.
Representatives from each of the English literature
classes came in groups. Dr. Kenjiro Umé came,
also newspaper-men. Father's face showed excite-
ment. After Mr. Umé had departed, father said:
'What a great heart that man has! What a fine
Japanese he is! He'll be a Prime Minister some
day. When I come before him, I feel like a mere
baby.' Thus he respected him, but Mr. Umé liked
saké (Japanese wine) and even when he was at his
desk writing, on one side of his desk would be a
cup of cold saké. Hearing this, father said, 'Oh, it
is very poisonous. It's risky; he will injure himself. It will take his life. If he loves his wife and

children, it's best to stop it. Stop it for the sake
of our country! I prayed for the man to live a long
time.' So saying, father used to be greatly troubled.

After that he was asked to be an instructor at
the Waseda University, and Dr. Takata, Dr.
Tsubouchi, Dr. Shiwozawa, and Professor Uchi-
gasaki all called on him, and father always seemed
to be in the best of spirits. After his return from
Waseda, father used to say, 'That University is
nothing like the governmental kind, and I like it
very much.' I asked him which was the more
splendid, Imperial University or Waseda University. Father took a fine gilt-edged, gilt-lettered
book from his desk and from a bookcase near-by a
yellow-covered plain book, and showing these two
together side by side, he said, 'If the big fine one
was Imperial University, then the yellow one is
Waseda.' 'Then,' I said, 'the Imperial University
is much grander, isn't it?' Father said: 'Fine
clothes do not always cover good character.
From the appearance of the cover, you cannot
judge the worth of the book. These two books —
look well and see what they are.' The big fine one
was an American catalogue of a certain bookstore.
The yellow one contained the thesis of some French
scholar, I believe.

One day father returned from the University
perspiring greatly, so mother said to him, 'You
must have exercised a great deal or got very much
excited.' He said: 'Today, I saw Count Ōkuma and

I advised him. It may have been better not to have said what I did, but when I saw him, I couldn't help doing so. It was about those foreign religious people who wear masks of religion, but in reality are offensive politicians. Be careful of them, I advised' — and he smiled.

Among us mischievous children, my brother Iwao received the most number of spankings from father. He had *okyū* several times applied to his body, but after a while he did not seem to mind them at all. Mother, who applied them, got discouraged and asked father to spank him. When he was scolded, Iwao would cry and tear around. This in fact was not to his gain. Sometimes one or two spankings would have settled the case; but for his kicking up he received more of them. At Ushigomé, Oroku would plead for us; at Yaidzu, Otokichi; at Ōkubo, the gardener or *jiiya*, who would apologize for us at such times. The year of father's death, father and mother were scolding Iwao. That day, when father was about to spank him, Iwao kicked up and kicked father on the chest. Father's face suddenly turned pale and afterward he said: 'I am getting old. The children are getting too big. My body is getting weak. Today, while scolding Iwao, I got very tired.' After that, when scolding Iwao, mother would always say, 'If you kick up again, I won't stand it. You kicked papa's breast; have you forgotten about it?' Kiyoshi was one day in a dangerous position on the cover of a well with other children, imitating the dance performed at one of the festivals, when grandmother discovered him. She reported it to mother, who asked father to spank him. After he was spanked, Kiyoshi cried so long and rubbed his eyes with his hands so much that he made the lids swell. Seeing this, father was worried and said to mother, 'There's no feeling so bad as after spanking the children. Every time I scold them, my life is shortened.'

The autumn after we moved to Ōkubo, I got the measles, then brother and mother contracted it. Brother's case was light, but for mother, who was thirty-five years old, and having it for the first time, it was trying. Father came to the head of our beds and said: 'If we are born to become human beings, we must go through this once, so keep as warm as possible and do as the doctor orders and you will surely get well. If you want anything, I will get it for you.' I at once took him at his word and asked for tin soldiers. Father said, 'All right,' and went out in a rickshaw, and returned after about two hours. He came in with bundles in both hands, from the contents of which came many regiments of soldiers, fine horses, fine wrestling groups. Of them all, the wrestling one was the most interesting. I kept it until I was about twenty years old.

One day, from the next lot we heard many men's voices and sounds of saws and chopping. When we looked out, we saw the fine trees swaying and branch after branch was cut off. Away up high was a man with a rope tied around his waist, working like a monkey. Seeing this going on, father was surprised. When the Kobudera trees were being cut down, father felt so bad that it hurt him as if they were cutting off his own hands and feet, and now to have to witness another miserable sight seemed as if opening up the wound again. 'Isn't there some means of saving the old trees on the lot next door?' We went at once to an old man who had lived for a long time in the neighbourhood and asked him to negotiate; but it was too late, all the old trees had been sold, so he couldn't break the contract now. There were so many that they could not be transplanted then. 'Can't you buy the land and take over the whole thing?' it was proposed. This place had five or six houses for rent, besides the trees, and if the part where the trees grew were bought it would leave only a long strip of land, so one would have to buy the houses also. Father had not the means to take them over. The trees towered up high in the sky; some were as old as two hundred or three hundred years and the youngest ones were at least fifty years or more. 'I would like to save you, but I can't! *Gomen, gomen* [pardon, pardon]. I am a miserable man — too poor — I can't save you — *gomen, gomen.*' He could not stand hearing the chopping and sawing going on, so he stayed away from home longer than usual on his walks.

Father disliked very much - to be seen off at the station or pier and to have great pomp shown by friends and relatives. He always said to mother: 'When I am leaving with Kazuo to go to America, don't see me off. Do as you always do when we go out for walks. Just see us off at the entrance with smiling faces, that is enough. If I should go to America, I will never send you a notice of the date of my arrival. I shall return suddenly, so you, mother, stay at home and be doing your favourite house-cleaning.' He frequently made such remarks to her. He even went on to say that, after he died, no notice was to be sent for some time to anyone. 'Put the bones in a jar worth about three sen and bury me in some temple on a hill.' When he had reached his fiftieth year, as the spirits of his departed friends began to increase, he felt keenly their loss and became more studious than ever. Two weeks before his death he felt the oppressive pain in his heart. Dr. Kizawa was sent for, and in the meantime he busied himself, writing hurriedly a letter to Dr. Umé in French, asking him to take charge of certain things in case of his death. But fortunately his ailment passed over. On this occasion, on hearing of father's illness, I was frightened and hurried with mother to his study. Father said very seriously, as if handing down to her his will, 'You must not think your body is your own. Your body is a treasure entrusted to you for the children, so please don't overstrain yourself.'

For two or three days previous to Monday, September 26, 1904, it had been dull cloudy weather. On this day, in the morning, it was unusually cold. 'Oh, what bad weather! This will kill me!' father said. None of us realized how soon his words were to be realized, so we laughed it off. 'Let us light a stove today,' father said. Before going to school, I went to father as usual to say, 'Papa, now I am going to school; good-bye'; but this time, without knowing what I was saying, I said instead, 'Good night, pleasant dreams.' Father replied, 'The same to you, darling, good night.' Father and son unconsciously exchanged the night greeting. Mother, hearing us, scolded and said, 'Why, it's morning.' Father and I looked at each other and laughed. This same day a letter came from Captain Fujisaki at the front, saying: 'I pray for the health of the whole family. I am alive and well. The war is taking a favourable turn. If you have some new interesting novels or dramas, please send them to me. If I am blessed with life, I shall return them to you. I am now on the reception committee to the foreign military observers. I look forward to receiving mail from you all, while listening to the roaring of the cannons in Manchuria.' Father wrote a reply at once (this was his last letter to anyone), and gave instructions that Maeterlinck's dramatic works be wrapped and sent to him. Then, for my dictation lesson, he had me write an English letter to Fujisaki-san.

For two or three days grandmother had been laid up with fever due to stomach trouble. Father said that, as there was a sick person in the house, it was not necessary to go to the trouble of preparing regular meals. Simple things would do — so he had only bread and milk. After the meal was over, brother Iwao was writing in simple Japanese a letter to Captain Fujisaki. I had a copy-book and was writing Japanese characters. Mother was with grandmother, as her fever was high, and was nursing her. That evening about eight o'clock, father, with a strange expression on his face, came down to our room (this room was a combination of children's room and dining-room), and opening the closet, asked the maid where the whiskey was. Ohana, the maid, called mother at once, and she left grandmother's sick-room and came. 'Oh, mamma — that trouble has returned again,' and father pressed his chest. He poured out a quarter of a cup of whiskey, filled it with water, and drank it, then went sadly down the

hall to his study. Mother went after him, but he
told her that he was all right. 'Now, you stay
by grandma or stay with the children.' He tried
to prevent her coming, but nevertheless she went
with him to his room. At the time, our maid
Ohana said, 'Master is quite bad — his face is
very pale.' She told me it might be necessary to
call Dr. Kizawa. 'Yes, I will go at once,' I said,
and while I was putting away the copy-book and
paper, my five-year-old brother Kiyoshi said,
'*Obāsama* [grandma] sick, papa sick, *iya, iya nē*'
(how unpleasant, unpleasant). After leaving the
desk, I went out into the hall. Just then mother
called out from father's room, 'Kazuo! Kazuo!
Ohana! all come at once!' Mother called out so
excitedly that saying 'Yes,' I was by father the
next moment, and touching his thick breast cried
out, 'Papa! Papa!' How I got there or how I ran
I have no remembrance; all I know is that I put
my hands on father's breast and cried out. It
was like a dream. His grey-haired moustache —
his lips so like a woman's — his lips opened a
little showing the tobacco-stained, irregular black
teeth, which were tightly closed. No voice or
breath came therefrom. From the high, aristo-
cratic nose, not a breath as small as an insect
came out. The big eyes were half open and the
balls turned upward. The eyes were lighted only
by the dim lamp. The white hair over his forehead
did not move a bit. With his two hands clasped

over his breast, he was lying on his back quietly. Crying out near his ear and shaking him by the chest, I got no reply, nor any movement. Sighing, he frequently used to say: 'It's hard for me to wait. Life is not long for me.' Thus father's words came back as a reality. It was not a dream. Father really was no more. He was dead, but so young and so suddenly. I never imagined that he would go like this. On father's desk was a manuscript partly written and at the side of it a pen, the ink on which had not yet dried. One door of the bookcase was open — today for my lesson, he had taken out a natural-history book to show me a certain picture and had failed to close it afterward. 'Ah, on account of sickness,' father said, and lay down on his bed and he died, so mother said.

Since the age of gods men have tried to understand and have gone astray; each, uttering his groans or shouting, has come to an end and passed away. Among these multitudes of people, twenty-six years ago, father Hearn, anxious about his wife and children, worrying about the accumulation of many things which he wished to write about, clasping his hands over his chest and uttering these pathetic words, 'Ah, on account of sickness!' — with these sad words on his lips, he passed out into the other world. Born into this world, he first learned Greek, was brought up to speak English, was taught French, Latin, and Spanish; this Hearn on his deathbed uttered, '*Ah, byōki no tamé*' (Ah, on account of sickness) regretfully, resignedly, left his final utterance in Japanese — died as a Japanese. Thus did Hearn pass away.

THE END